"History is not just stone, notable people, and bricks. It includes the reaction of those who were there and the community's ongoing response."

—Jim Boles

Vanishing Past Series

This is book is #4 of the Vanishing Past Series published by Vanishing Past Press LLC. Vanishing Past Press is dedicated to the documentation, preservation, and distribution of works of scholarship and cultural importance with emphasis on under-examined or unexplored topics.

This book is part of that effort.

Note on visiting the historic locations:
Many of the historic locations are on private property and you may need permission to visit; often there will be posted signs.

WHEN THERE WERE POORHOUSES
Early Care in Rural New York 1808–1950

James M. Boles, Ed.D

ABANDONED HISTORY

Copyright © 2016 reassigned to James M. Boles, 2022

ISBN: 978-0-9845983-3-5

All rights reserved No part of this publication may be reproduced, stored in a retrieval system, or transmitted in any form by any process, electronic, mechanical, photocopying, recording, or otherwise without the permission of the copyright owner. For reprint permission please contact jamesboles47@gmail.com

Publisher: Vanishing Past Press, LLC
Technical Advisor: Carolyn Ryder
Layout Artist: Rachel Bridges Design

Cover image: Odd Fellows Orphan Home, 299 Old Niagara Road, Lockport, New York

To the volunteers, human service workers, board members, charity agencies, and government organizations who all contribute, each in their own way, to help people in need.

James M. Boles EdD

About This Book

Jim Boles Ed.D is a retired CEO of People Inc., a health and human service agency in Western New York., and has worked in helping agencies for over 50 years. He is the founder of the Museum of disABILITY History in Amherst, New York. When There Were Poor Houses, is a series of research-based articles many previously published in the *Lockport, New York, Union Sun and Journal*, and the *Niagara Falls Gazette*, Niagara Falls, New York, the articles have been updated for this publication. His research interests include early care and healing, and local history with a focus on Western New York. Boles has a strong interest in preserving the area's history and promoting cultural tourism. He works out of the corporate headquarters of Vanishing Past Press- which is located at one end of his family room.

Dedicated to the citizens of Western New York who care, the readers of hometown newspapers, local historians, historical societies and libraries. All are strong and a great resource.

1

INTRODUCTION 1

1808–1860
- 1808 Outdoor Relief and Other Help............................11
- 1829 The Almshouse on Poor House Road..................17
- 1837 Henry Wells Speech School..................................35
- 1850s Poorhouses* of the German Settlements.............41
- 1852 Pest Houses of Niagara County...........................49
- 1857 DeVeaux School for Orphan and
  Destitute Children..65
- 1857 School for Colored Deaf, Dumb, and
  Blind Children...77

Unless otherwise noted on maps or in historical quotes, "poorhouse" will be used throughout.

2

1870s–1906
- 1871 Home for the Friendless and Wyndham
  Lawn Home for Children....................................93
- 1888 Flagler Hospital..105
- 1890 Fort Niagara Hospital...111
- 1891 Lockport Charity Organization Society..............117
- 1893 The Provident Wood Yard Mission and
  Day Care...121
- 1894 Independent Order of Odd Fellows Homes........125
- 1895 Charity Organization Society, Niagara Falls........137
- 1904 Villa St. Vincent..147
- 1906 Niagara Falls Quarantine Hospital
  (Municipal Hospital)..157

3

1908–1918
- 1908 Stella Niagara...169
- 1908 Buffalo State Hospital Wilson Farm Colony........175
- 1915 Niagara County Infirmary –
  The "New" County Poorhouse............................183
- 1918 Niagara County Tuberculosis Hospital................193
- 1918 The Byron V. Covert Quarantine Hospital..........205

4 1920s–1950

- 1922 The Charity Club, Lockport, New York.............217
- 1928 Niagara County Health Camp........................221
- 1929 St. Mary's Home for Children.......................233
- 1930 The Martha H. Beeman Foundation Child Guidance Clinics...243
- 1931 St. Francis of Mt. Alvernia Summer Camp..........247
- 1933 St. Mary's School for the Deaf, Vocational Farm School for Boys..255
- 1939 "The Boys Home," Barker, New York, A Residential Boys School....................................263
- 1950 Sunshine League for Retarded Children and Niagara County Chapter of the Association for the Help of Retarded Children......................267

5 PROGRAMS BEYOND NIAGARA COUNTY

Large Specialized Institutions Beyond Niagara County...274

Notes..285
Acknowledgments...293
Bibliography..297
Definitions...301
Illustration and Photo Credits.............................307
Index..313

Introduction

New York's history of caring for the poor, elderly, and disabled began while it was still a colony of the British Empire and continued throughout the twentieth century. A wide range of helping services and institutions were created, and some—under different names and settings—are still operating today. As societal needs and attitudes changed and knowledge evolved, many institutions merged, reorganized, or closed their doors forever.

The history of abandoned almshouses, poorhouses, orphanages, and pest houses, for example, often lies buried among the neglect of time, much like the unmarked graves found at many institutions.

The helping services offered in Niagara County, a typical rural county of New York State, are illustrative of the way the needy, poor and disabled were cared for in the past. In this book, the author uses the institutions of Niagara County as an example to capture the abandoned history of social services.

Niagara County is located in the northwestern corner of New York State. "Niagara" is derived from the Seneca word *Onguiaahra*, meaning "thunder of waters." It is bordered on the north by Lake

Ontario, on the west by the Niagara River, on the south by Erie County and the Buffalo metropolitan area, and on the east by Orleans and Genesee Counties. Niagara County was formed in 1808 by subdivision from Genesee County.

In 1821 Niagara County was subdivided again when the New York Legislature formed two counties—Erie and Niagara—out of the old Niagara County. The famous Niagara Falls and the thirty-six-mile-long Niagara River runs along the northwest border into Lake Ontario, separating the United States and Canada. Soon after the completion of the Erie Canal, Niagara County opened its first helping facility, the Niagara County Almshouse, to serve poor, aged, orphaned, and disabled residents.

Niagara County was an ideal region to research early programs. In Niagara you see a smaller view of the care provided in most of the more populated counties of New York State. All were dealing with rapid growth, new developments like the Erie Canal, and a growing population of immigrants. Niagara County, like much of the United States, was changing from a farming economy to a manufacturing economy.

If you lived in Niagara County in the mid-twentieth century, you were aware of the special help offered in large buildings set back from the road that were for people in need of assistance. Children could go to Wyndham Lawn Orphan Home in Lockport, but the wayward were warned about a possible visit to Father Baker's Orphan Home in Lackawanna or the dark stone buildings of DeVeaux Orphan/Military School in Niagara Falls. There were still remnants of the large Niagara County Poorhouse on Davison Road in Lockport as well as the nearby pauper's graveyard. Mount View Hospital in the Town of Lockport and its ever-changing role as a facility for people in need stood proudly on a hill.

This book considers the more visible institutions and also uncovers the history of lesser known helping services in Niagara County. The main focus of this book is on special needs programs from 1808 through 1950, including schools, orphan homes, poorhouses, pest houses, and special hospitals or hospital units. As the system matured, more specialized services developed in other areas of New York State; the best examples of these institutions are highlighted to track the progression of care.

Through years of research and experience the author brings to light the records and facilities of past helping programs that were abandoned with little documentation or local institutional memory. In the helping fields, care moves on. The past is quickly forgotten, often denied, and there is much easy criticism of previous efforts. This historical focus leads to a narrow perspective as practices involving care and treatment evolve. Much of the historical research into earlier care in the almshouses, orphanages, and other institutions is negative. Early philosophies can seem dated and perhaps harsh, but at the time the care was given it was often the only and best available.

The programs described here were started to help those in need: the poor, the sick, the orphans, and the disabled. Most were funded by the government, a charity or religious group,

Niagara County Population
1820..............22,990
1840..............31,132
1870..............50,437 (11,260 foreign)
1920..............118,705
1950..............189,992

The census in Niagara County over 130 years reveals periods of growth, placing burdens on local towns and villages to care for people in need. Niagara County census information taken from the Niagara and Orleans Counties atlas published by Beers, Upton and Company, New York, and the U.S. Census Bureau.

or through a combination of efforts. Consequently, a blend of social and moral values influenced the overall direction of the service. Care providers' concerns were often the same as those of the local community, as true in 1829 as it is today, with both positive and negative outcomes. If anything, a look back at this early assistance shows that methods always change.[1] History reveals that as the need for care of the poor, the sick, children, and the disabled increased, Niagara County residents and their government responded.[2,3]

The intent of my research was to document these early efforts. Many of these organizations are forgotten and the buildings they operated in were destroyed. However, a surprising number of facilities still exist, sometimes housing similar programs. A look back at these early institutions reveals that there have always been people who need assistance, and the history of that assistance is all around us. That old stone house on Market Street in Lockport, New York, was once a well-known sanitarium. The store front on Locust Street in Lockport was an early school for disabled children. A school for orphans once stood on what is now a state park in Niagara Falls, New York.

Research in Niagara County uncovered more than thirty locations where help was given and there are many more. Future research could involve facilities for the elderly and both public and private schools. Sanitariums, some of which employed very colorful treatments, are another interesting group of institutions. Primarily located in Niagara Falls and Lockport, sanitariums operated from the mid-nineteenth until well into the early twentieth century.

For this publication, we include only programs between 1808 and the 1950s that were significant during the time they functioned and for which sufficient information was available to tell their stories. Many organizations ran notable programs that fell outside these guidelines. The importance of the religious and benevolent groups in the care for the poor, disabled, elderly, and children, as well as the contribution of women's groups and religious women, has yet to be fully recognized.

I encourage readers to contact the author with corrections or new information that may be useful as this material is updated for reference. As you drive the roads of Western New York, this book will help identify the former locations and existing structures of some unique and special programs that helped those in need.

As you learn about history remember: "The past is a foreign country: they do things differently there," L.P. Hartley.

Let find out "what were they thinking."

—Jim Boles

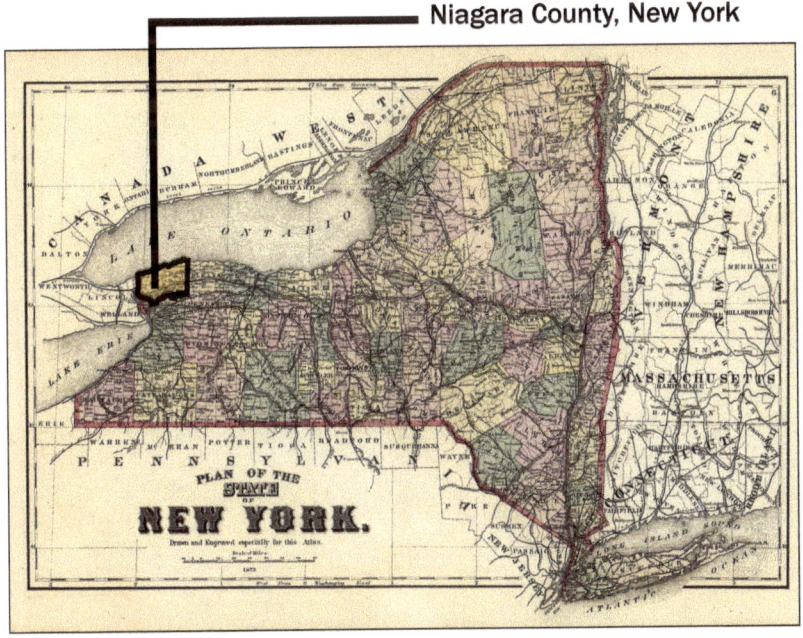

Niagara County, New York

Editor's note: The exact language of the historical periods researched for this book is retained for historical accuracy. No offense is intended toward any individual or group.

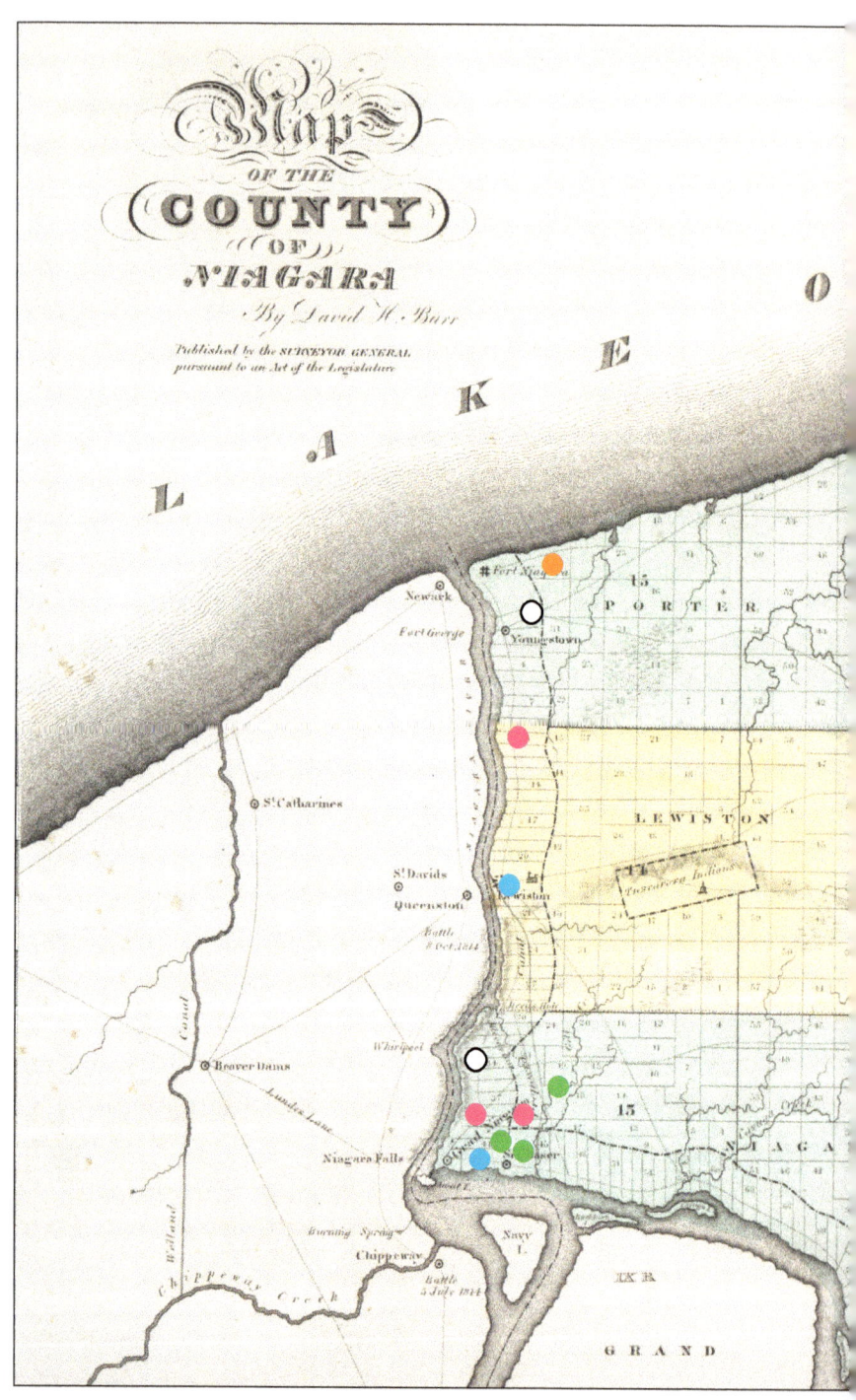

County of Niagara, 1839.

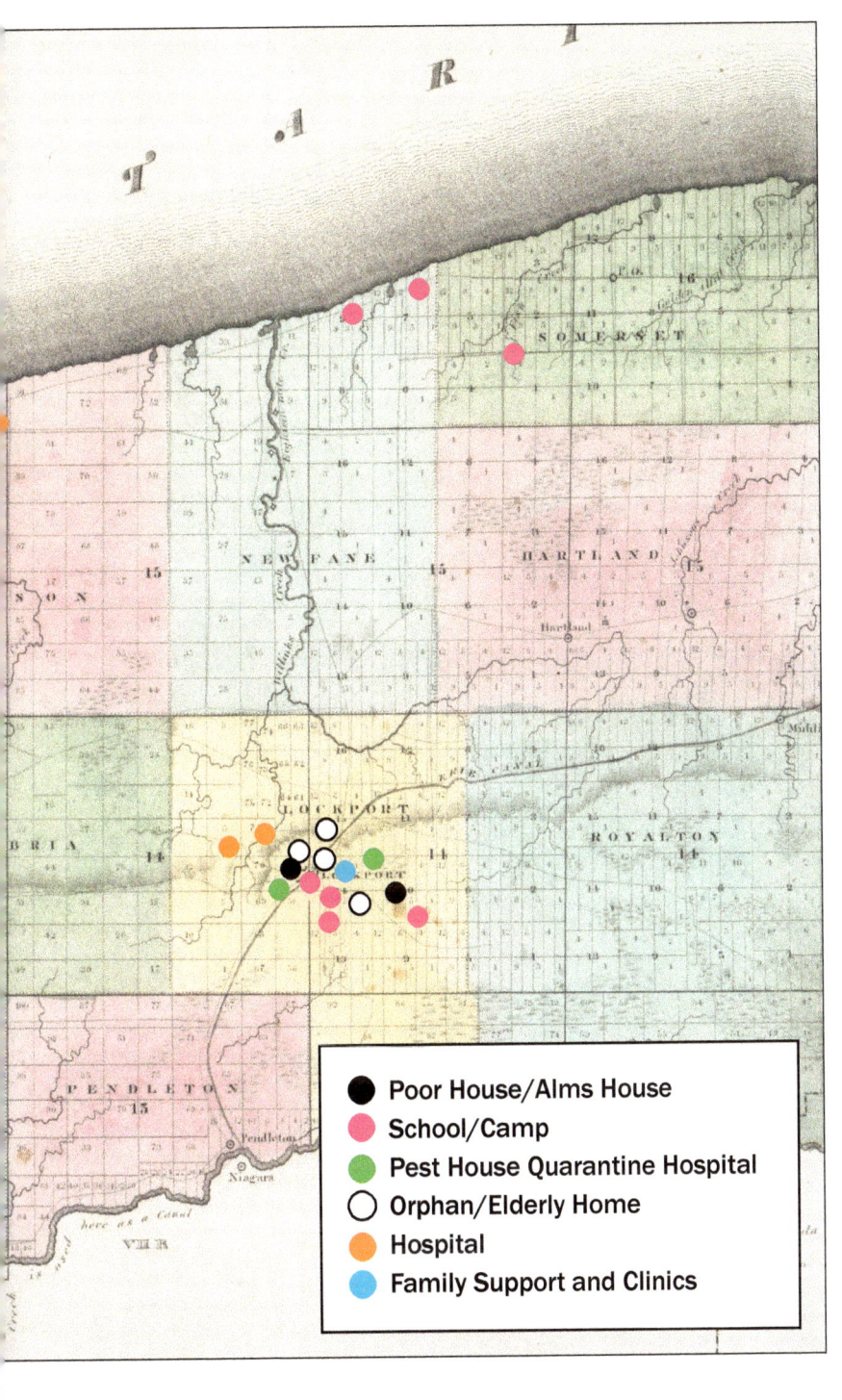

CHAPTER 1
1808-1860

Outdoor Relief and Other Help

The first governmental action on behalf of people who were poor, elderly, and disabled in Niagara County was the establishment of a special position in each town to administer government funds that provided support for the needy. Every town appointed an overseer of the poor or poor master to supervise what was generally called outdoor relief. Such help might, for example, consist of coal for the winter or lodging at a farm or boarding house. Most of the residents in need were assisted with relief instead of being sent to the county poorhouse.

A good example of outdoor relief is found in the town of Lewiston, which created an office of the poor in 1818. The Lewiston Historical Society has later records created by Augustus Hause, overseer of the poor from 1878-1879. Such records provide compelling glimpses into the past.

Almshouse or poorhouse
A place operated by the local government or a charity to house needy or dependent persons.

Outdoor relief for George Rewey and his family ranged from flour and "goods" to physician's services. Overseer of the poor record book, 1879, Lewiston.

> **Outdoor Relief**
> Assistance, in the form of money, food, clothing or goods, given to alleviate poverty without the requirement that the recipient enter an institution. In contrast, recipients of indoor relief were required to enter a workhouse or poorhouse.

One entry notes: "For Lewiston-Niagara, George Rewey – born in U.S. – has wife and three children all living with him – is a cripple and not able to do hard labor – has been assisted from the poor fund of Lewiston since October 1, 1878."

George Rewey was likely injured in a farm or industrial accident. Typical entries in the overseer's book described basic provisions to the Rewey family. George Rewey was carried on the books for only two years. Often, the last entry noted about recipients of aid was for medical care: On September 23, 1879, the final entry for the Rewey family lists a $14.50 charge for physician services.

There were many organizations that provided help for those in need. Their history is not thoroughly documented but glimpses surface in occasional newspaper articles or interviews. For example, the members of the Sacarissa Odd Fellows Lodge in Lewiston followed the Odd Fellows Creed "to improve and elevate the character of mankind…to visit the sick, relieve the distressed, bury the dead and educate the orphaned."

The lodge was founded in 1846. Historical records show an active "Widows and Orphan fund" and many donations to help

> *There were many organizations that provided help for those in need. Their history is not thoroughly documented but glimpses surface in occasional newspaper articles or interviews.*

the unfortunate. According to the bylaws of the lodge, "fees and dues will provide for a widow and orphan's fund, an education fund and a funeral tax...every member (in good standing) in case of sickness or disability, bodily accident or mental infirmity shall be entitled to and receive weekly benefits."

> " It is one of the fundamentals of our Order to develop men into good citizens, good fathers, good husbands, good brothers...We are nothing more than creatures of environment; helpless, mere feathers driven by the wind, unless we can interweave our strength with that of others and together make a determined and successful stand against the adverse forces of life."
>
> From the Album of Odd Fellows Homes, published about 1908.

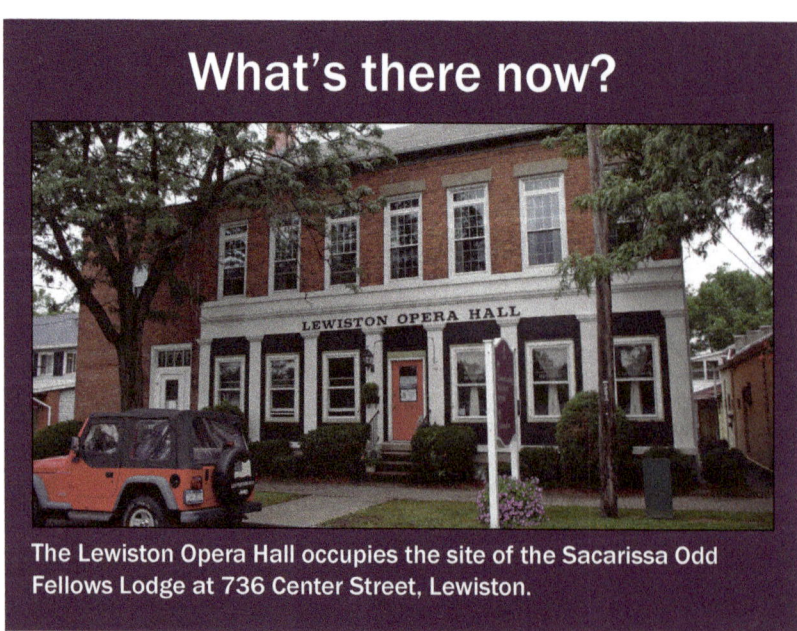

The Lewiston Opera Hall occupies the site of the Sacarissa Odd Fellows Lodge at 736 Center Street, Lewiston.

The Almshouse on Poor House Road Lockport, New York 1829–1915

Niagara Street Extension and Gothic Hill Road

In 1824 New York State established an almshouse law that required each county to build an almshouse or poorhouse to care for those who were unable to care for themselves. Almshouses—the first form of institutional help— typically cared for people who were poor, sick, homeless, mentally ill, injured, or considered mentally deficient. There were no specialized facilities such as nursing homes or institutions for people with special needs.[1]

Niagara County established an almshouse in Lockport in 1829. Additional land was purchased in 1854. The grounds spread across both sides of Niagara Street Extension and eventually continued to Upper Mountain Road, where the Niagara County Sanatorium was later built. Early maps and descriptions indicate that Niagara Street Extension had several names, including Gulf Road or Poor House Road. Gothic Hill Road was also known as Poor House Hill. The property included the home, and 120 acres of land.

Over the 86 years it was open the Poorhouse had a total of five hospitals (depending what you count as a hospital). In 1845

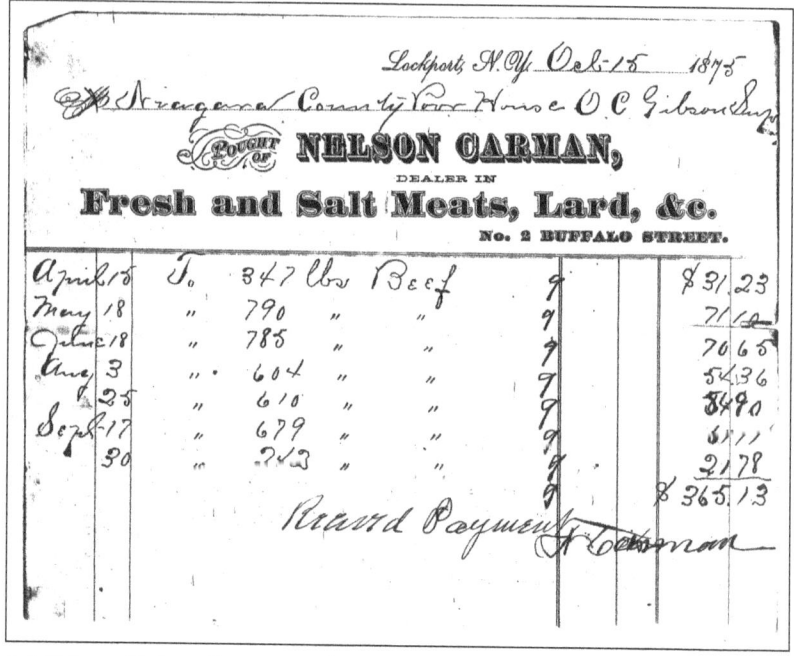

A bill from Nelson Carman, a Lockport merchant, 1875.

Niagara County Almshouse (Poorhouse) History

1829: The first building was erected and opened in the fall of the same year. It was described as a "commodious frame dwelling."

1833: A large main building of fieldstone with dimensions of 100' x 60' was built.

1834: The almshouse school was operating. David Murphy was the first teacher. Local children from the area attended school with children from the almshouse.

> **KEEPER OF THE COUNTY POOR-HOUSE WANTED**
> -- The Superintendents of the Poor of the county of
> Niagara, hereby give notice: That they will receive
> sealed proposals for keeping the Poor House from the
> first day of April next. Keeper and family to be boarded
> at the expense of the county. Proposals should state
> the terms per year, his age and occupation, the number
> of children, their ages and the number of years he will
> continue at the same rate. Proposals will be received
> by either of the Superintendents, and until the 1st day
> of January inst., on which day the Superintendents
> will meet at their office in the P.H. to examine such
> proposals.
>
> Jan. 6.   4w   W. PARSONS, Cl'k

An advertisement in the *Niagara Democrat* seeking a keeper for the Niagara County "Poor-House," January 6, 1837.

1845: Two three-story additions were added to the main building. One of the additions was for the "insane."

1852: The pest house, a stone building 14' x 24', was built on the grounds.

1854: An additional twenty-nine acres of land was annexed to the ninety-one-acre property, totaling 120 acres.

1858: A "crazy yard" was built, enclosed by a nine-foot-tall stone wall, and used for residents with mental health issues.

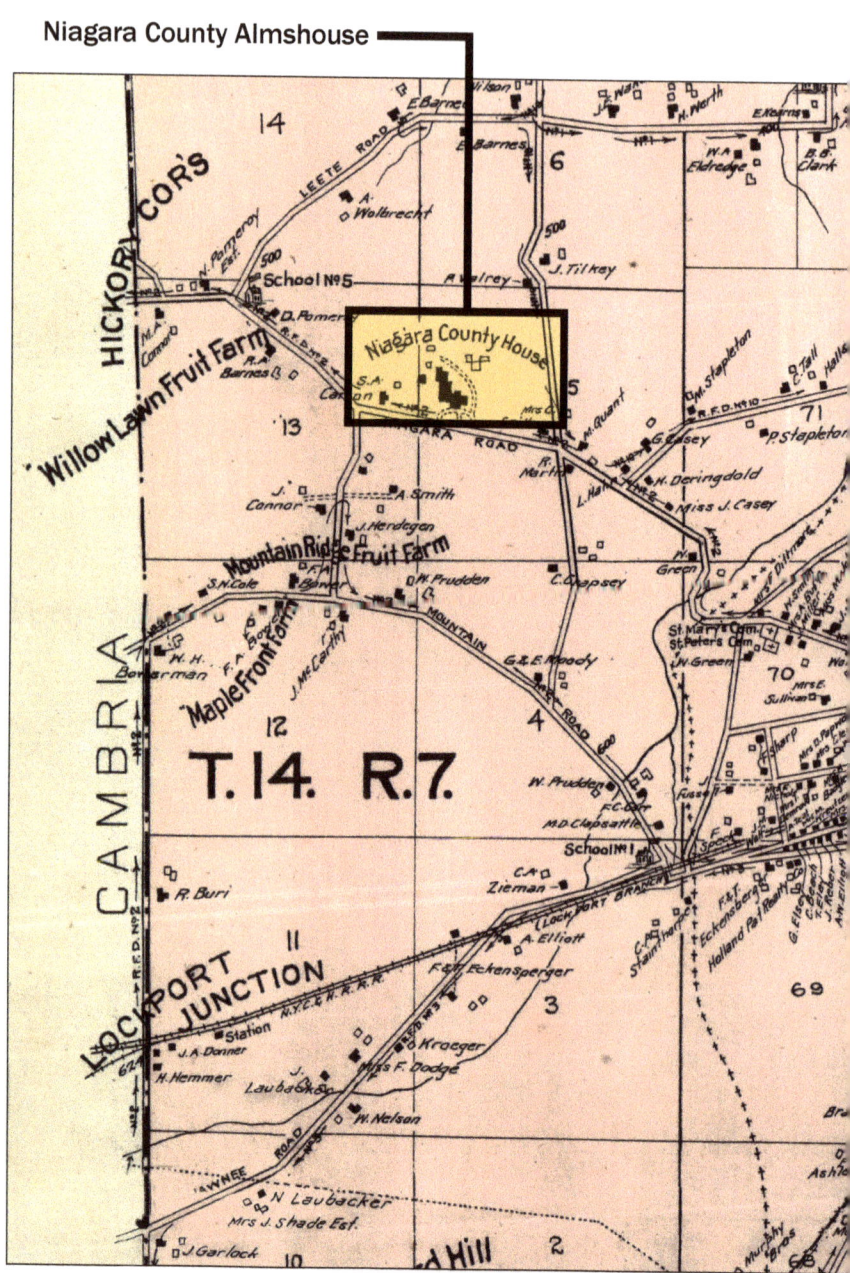

Niagara County Almshouse, Town of Lockport, 1908.

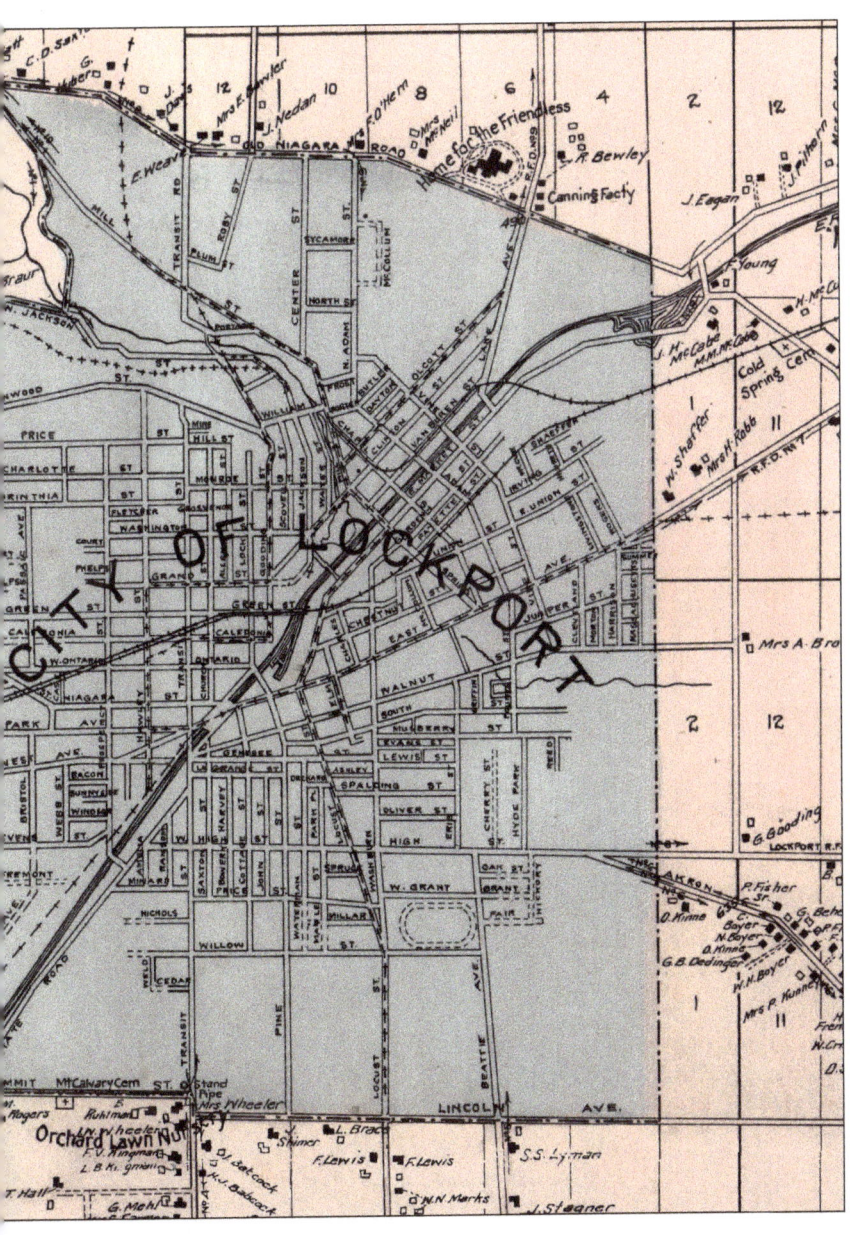

18 POOR HOUSE STATISTICS—POST OFFICES & POST MASTERS.

COUNTY POOR HOUSE STATISTICS.

The number of inmates of the Poor House October 1, 1867, was	140
Number admitted during the year	231
Born during the year	4
Whole number discharged	242
Number remaining Sept. 30, 1868	133

The causes of pauperism are reported as follows:

Sickness	61
Destitution	52
Insanity	7
Intemperance	54
Orphanage	27
Cripples	12
Blind	6
Old age	12
Born in Poor House	4
The average number of paupers in the Poor House for the year ending September 30, 1868	199
Average expense per week each	$1.85

As documented in this 1867–68 report, just before the Home for the Friendless in Lockport was organized, twenty-seven orphans were cared for in the almshouse.

1860: A new addition was added to the west side of the almshouse.

1870s: Specialized facilities for children, the mentally ill, deaf, the mentally retarded, and blind were established outside of the almshouse.

1915: The almshouse closed and the hospital building was used for the county's first tuberculosis hospital.

> "We proceeded to inspect the ruins of the old Poor House barn. An interview over the phone a few days later with Mr. Collopy who now owns the farm and whose house is across the Niagara St. Ext. from the new jail, elicited considerable information. He told me the Poor House had been directly back of his house...he remembers the padded cells where the insane patients were kept, and thinks they were approximately six by eight feet. In these small cells in the basement of one wing of the Poor House were confined the pauper lunatics. A yard 100 feet square was surrounded by a stone wall nine feet high. This connected with the basement and was known as the 'crazy yard', it being used for the less violent patients to exercise. Occasionally as many as three patients were kept in one cell and several poormasters reported they could not keep the cells comfortably warm in winter because of inadequate heating facilities. In 1863 there were 35 lunatics crowded into the cells. In 1865 a State Insane Asylum at Utica took over the care of the insane from this county."

September 30, 1960 article in the Lockport Union-Sun and Journal. *Niagara County Historian, Clarence O. Lewis describes his exploration of the Old Poor House Farm.*

1916–1930s: The remaining building and farm were used by the county for the Niagara Industrial Prison Farm.

1917: The hospital building was moved to the Niagara Sanatorium property.

1960: Niagara County Jail was built on part of the property. When crews prepared the site for construction, graves were found on what was believed to be the burial ground for the old pest house.

Inmates of the Niagara County Poor House laws of 1875						
Record #	Date	Name	Sex	Age	Color	Remarks
937	1894	Simon Gould	M	11	White	Orphan-sent to Limestone Hill Buffalo
929	1916	Carolyn Byam	F	80	White	Old and Destitute
1495	1885	Jos Overhauser	M			8 Overhauser Children
1507	1885	Catherine "	F			Father and Mother died
1508	1885	Peter "	M			Sent to the following facilities
1509	1885	John "	M			German R.C.O. (A) Asylum
1510	1885	Francis "	M			Edward St. Asylum - Catholic
1511	1885	Chas "	M			Protectory (Buffalo N.Y.)
1512	1885	Charles "	M			Home of Friendless
1512½	1885	William "	M			(Lockport N.Y.)
1238	1883	Tho Johnson	M	50	Black	Sick, Lame and Destitute, Died February 19, 1883
1532	1885	Lillie Reed	F	6	White	Bound to Mary A. Lewis Discharged July 27, 1885
1536	1885	Phineus S. Ely	M	40		Married, First Class Lawyer Insane and Destitute, Hard Drinking
1713	1917	Rosanna Jann	F	63		Cancer of the breast

Sample Records of the Niagara County Poor House 1883-1917
Note _____X_____ Museum of disABILITY History
Poor House Records

A list of "inmates" from Niagara County Almshouse records.

An 1857 document known as the Yates Report provided a good overview of the operations of the Niagara County Almshouse:

> This consists of a stone building seventy-five by forty feet, three stories; another thirty by forty feet, two stories; connected with a farm of one hundred and twenty acres, yielding an annual revenue of $1,000...The superintendents of the poor, through the keeper, procures the supplies, prescribes rules regulating the diet, binds out the children, and exercises the power of discharging lunatics...During the last year there have been five births and thirteen deaths.
>
> The measles has prevailed among the children, three or four of whom died. This establishment is one of the few that has a pest house. Of the inmates nineteen are lunatics--six male and thirteen female--and all but three are paupers; of those three, one is a man worth from $6,000 to $7,000 placed here by his friends because they were denied admission into the State Asylum; another, a lady worth still more, placed here by her friends; and a third, a girl, placed here by her father. Thirty lunatics have been admitted during the year. They are under the care of a young physician, assisted by a female attendant. None are confined unless at night, and only one restrained (a negro) by shackles to keep him from running away; he is constantly employed on the farm, and is an efficient hand, and seemed happy. During the year five have been cured and discharged, and two much improved. It will be observed that in this house, as in all others where any proper attention is bestowed upon the insane, happy results follow. Four of the inmates are idiots, all males, two boys 12, and two 16 years of age; two are blind.[2]

Hospital under construction, 1899-1900.

Barn for farming operations. The barn foundation and dirt ramp remain on the property today.

a wing and a courtyard was built for people with mental illness. A quarantine hospital(Pest House) was first mentioned in 1852 and another one in 1864. Hospitals constructed in 1861 and 1871 are mentioned in documents, finally a new hospital was built in 1899. Early in Niagara County history there were no official public hospitals. Some doctor's offices functioned as small hospitals. Niagara Falls had a few sanitariums and a public quarantine hospital in 1893. Fort Niagara had a hospital that was used by the community(1890). There is mention of Dr. Isaac Smith in Lockport having some boarding capacity in the 1830's.

Because of nature of who they served, with the old, sick, injured and disabled making up a large percentage of their population, much of the facility was like a care home. It evolved to serve many needy groups.

The Poorhouse Closes

As the nineteenth century came to a close, the Niagara County Almshouse was in such disrepair that it needed to be replaced. A November 1908 report from the official record of the Niagara County Supervisor's Office reviewed a State Charities Report noting:

> This almshouse, with its old, decayed interior, poorly arranged, dark and inconvenient, is not a worthy memorial of the charitable instincts, enlightenment and generosity of the people of Niagara County. It should be replaced by a group of new buildings, or thoroughly remodeled.

The review came years before the county built the Niagara County Infirmary in 1915 on Davison Road and the Niagara Sanatorium (Mount View Hospital) in 1918 on Upper Mountain Road, both in Lockport. These two facilities replaced the old almshouse on Niagara Street Extension. After the poorhouse moved in 1915 to Davison Road, the county's committee on county buildings recommended "that the old county poor farm shall hereafter be known and called the Niagara [Prison] Industrial Farm...[and] that the building be put in reasonable repair." The report recommends obtaining help from prisoners at the Niagara County Jail.

Flooding and drainage problems on the property contributed to the decision to move the almshouse to Davison Road. The land was difficult to farm and much of it was rocky. After the

The first Niagara County Almshouse, Niagara Street Extension, Lockport.

> In 1896 Dad was offered a job as a farm boss at the County House at $20 a month. The following spring we moved to the corner of Crapsey Road and Niagara Road (now Sunset Drive and Niagara Extension). Our activities centered around the County House. They had a beautiful yard and we often went over and played croquet. I enjoyed gathering wild strawberries and blackberries and watching a bluebird that came back and made her nest in the same hollow of the apple tree every year."

Excerpt from the memoir of Ruth McGowan Taylor, 1977.[3]

move, county supervisor records show that the old buildings were maintained by the prison farm. Later, a contract was awarded to level the buildings, but it is uncertain whether this was fully completed.

An article in the Lockport *Union-Sun and Journal* dated Friday, September 30, 1960, mentioned that land owner Nelson Collopy used stone from the poorhouse to build up his driveway, likely because of persistent water problems.

The original almshouse property served Niagara County in three final roles. The hospital became the county's first tuberculosis hospital in 1915. The buildings and property were used for the Niagara Industrial Prison Farm in 1917, and the county jail was built on the former poorhouse grounds in 1960.

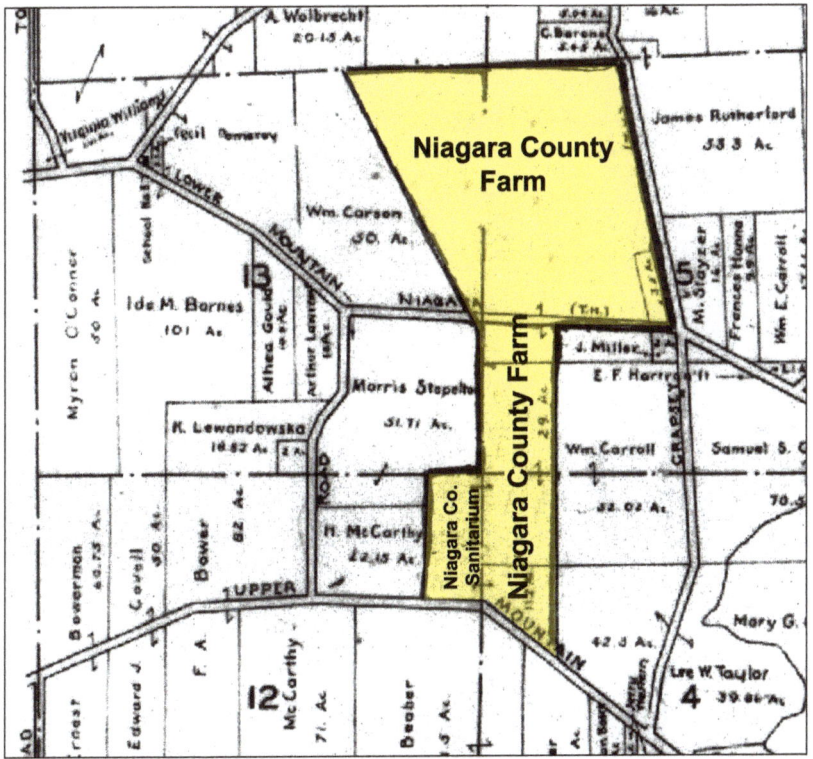

Town of Lockport, Niagara County, 1936.

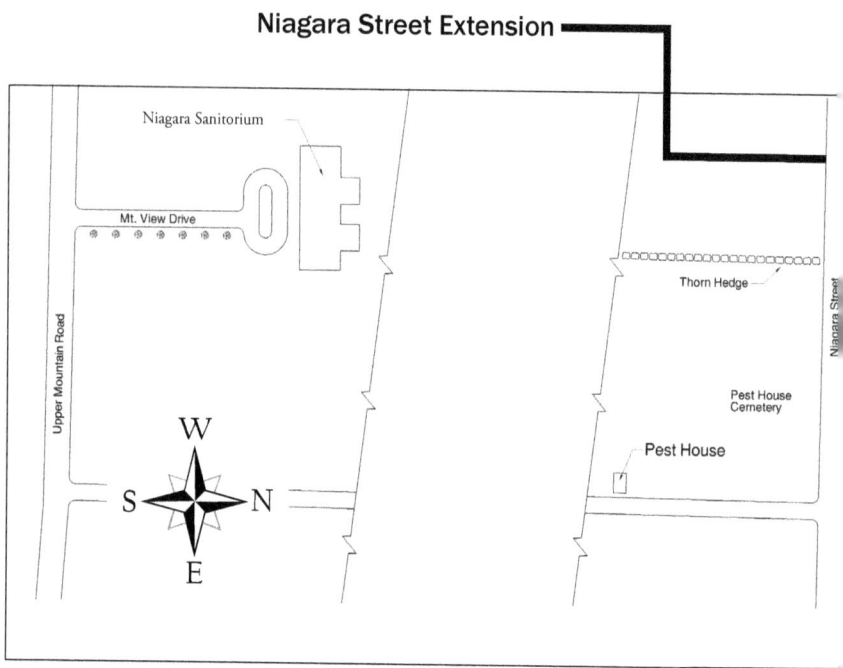

Site plan for the old almshouse and Niagara Sanatorium.

Poor House Records

The Niagara County Historian's Office and the Niagara County History Association, both in Lockport, New York have partial early records. New York State Archives have access to a searchable on-line data base titled "New York, U.S. Census on Inmates in Almshouses and Poorhouses, 1830-1920". A project that I am working on, will have the available death records on a searchable spreadsheet ,which will be found at both the Niagara County Historian's Office and the Niagara County History Association.

The Poorhouse Cemetery on Niagara County Property

Approximately 1,400 people are buried in the poorhouse cemetery located in the northwest section of the Niagara County property.

1808-1860   31

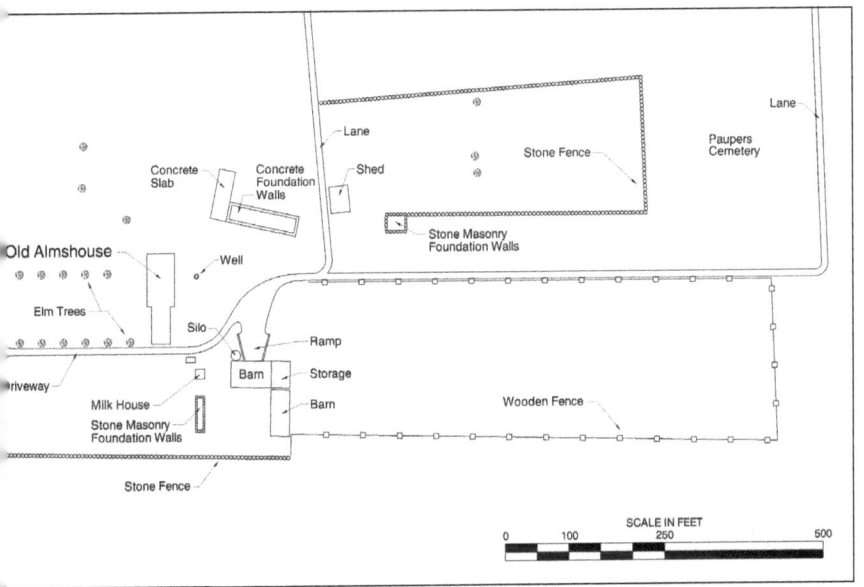

Bill Long Associates Architects, Buffalo, New York.

You can visit this graveyard. A right-of-way (see map - driveway) cuts through the brush to the right of the house, across from the present Niagara County Jail. The graveyard is to the left, just past the silo and barn foundation at the end of the right-of-way. The site is overgrown, and only a few dozen of the graves are marked with small stones and all are without names or numbers. An effort in 1993 resulted in the county re-purchasing the cemetery property. It is periodically cleared of brush, but most of it remains overgrown. I believe the burial ground may be larger than indicated.

The cemetery is small for over 1,400 burials. A recently discovered book of burial records lists up to three bodies buried in each grave. The book contains numbers for the lot and each grave, but there is no map to place the location of the graves. The only marked headstone in the poorhouse cemetery names members of a prominent Niagara County family and a freed slave.

The engraved stone records Sophia Wilson, wife of S. S. Merritt, born June 26, 1805, died Mar 27, 1864; Lewis W., son of S. S. and Sophia Merritt, born Oct 30, 1833, died May 22, 1865; and Louie Spencer, died July 20, 1884. Poorhouse records for Louie Spencer were found but not for Sophia and Lewis Merritt.

Sophia and Lewis Merritt's names were also engraved on the Merritt family gravestone in the Sawyer Homestead Cemetery in Newfane. All dates and names are the same, except Sophia's engraving, which lists "Willson" rather than "Wilson" as her maiden name. Their names appear together on Shubal S. Merritt's large gravestone. Shubal was Sophia's husband and Lewis was their son.

Accounts in the Merritt file at the Niagara County Historian's Office indicate that Sophia was visiting Niagara County and fell ill. Also, a Lewis Merritt death notice says he became ill in Cleveland and returned home to Niagara County and died. Further information from the Marjim Manor (family homestead -now a winery) records indicate that both Sophia and Lewis died of tuberculosis.

Although from a wealthy family, Sophia and Lewis Merritt may have been quarantined residents at the pest house. They died and were buried in graves at the almshouse—likely to protect their still healthy family members from infection. One of the two graves for Sophia and Lewis Merritt must be a cenotaph, the term for an empty tomb.

The third name on the stone is Louie Spencer. His death notice appeared in *The New York Times* on July 25, 1884. "Louis (Louie) Spencer, a black gentleman, died in the poorhouse in 1884. His age is listed as 115 years." The Spencer surname appears in Sophia Wilson Merritt's family history, so there may be a connection that explains the engraving of his information on the headstone.

A COLORED CENTENARIAN'S DEATH.

LOCKPORT, July 24.—Louis Spencer, better known as "Chuck-a-Luck," a colored man, who has for many years lived in Niagara County, died last night at the County Poor House of senile debility, his age, according to the most authentic records, being 115 years. He was probably the oldest person in the United States. In early life he was a slave in the South, and several years ago, before his memory failed, he could relate many interesting stories of his slavery days, and declared that he could remember the last days of the Revolutionary War. He was at one time a familiar figure at the different hotels throughout Niagara County.

From *The New York Times,* published July 25, 1884.

What's there now?

Merritt–Spencer stone in the old poorhouse cemetery.

Henry Wells Speech School
Eagle House, Main Street
Lockport, New York
1837

Henry Wells, a freight agent for the Erie Canal, lived in Western New York for a time and helped found American Express, Wells Fargo, and other businesses. Wells started several speech schools and Wells College for Women, in Aurora, New York. The Lockport speech school was advertised in the *Niagara Democrat* in 1837. Wells, who had speech problems, had developed an educational program for people who stuttered.

> Impediments of Speech - Mr. Wells, whose card will be found in another column, comes highly recommended for his success in curing impediments of speech. His is the principal of an Institution in New York, where stammering has been treated with unexampled success. His stay here for a short time, should induce the afflicted to give him a trial.

Article, *Niagara Democrat*, Lockport, New York, January 31, **1837**.

Eagle House, Henry Wells Speech School, was located just north of the "Big Bridge" on Main Street in Lockport in 1837. After a fire, the Eagle House was rebuilt. The hotel changed names several times. Here it is shown as Hotel Kenmore.

His speech school was located in rented rooms at the Eagle House Hotel on West Main and Canal Streets in Lockport.

The building went through several name changes, burned down, and was rebuilt as the Judson House. The last hotel at that location was the LOX Plaza, demolished in 1971. The Lockport Municipal Building is now located on the site.

A CARD

Mr. Editor: - I wish through the medium of your columns, to give notice to persons afflicted with stammering or stuttering, that an opportunity is now offered them of being cured, with little trouble and comparatively trifling expense. Having received an invitation from several persons in this village, I have taken rooms and opened a school at the Eagle Tavern, where I could receive a few more pupils if immediate application is made, as I shall teach but one class here. Terms will be made known on application to the subscriber, at his room, No. 46, second story, between the hours of 10 A.M. and 4 P.M. A cure in all cases guarantied, or the money will be refunded. Ladies will be taught in a separate class if requested.

HENRY WELLS

Niagara Democrat, Lockport, January 31, 1837.

Portrait of young Henry Wells

Henry Wells

What's there now?

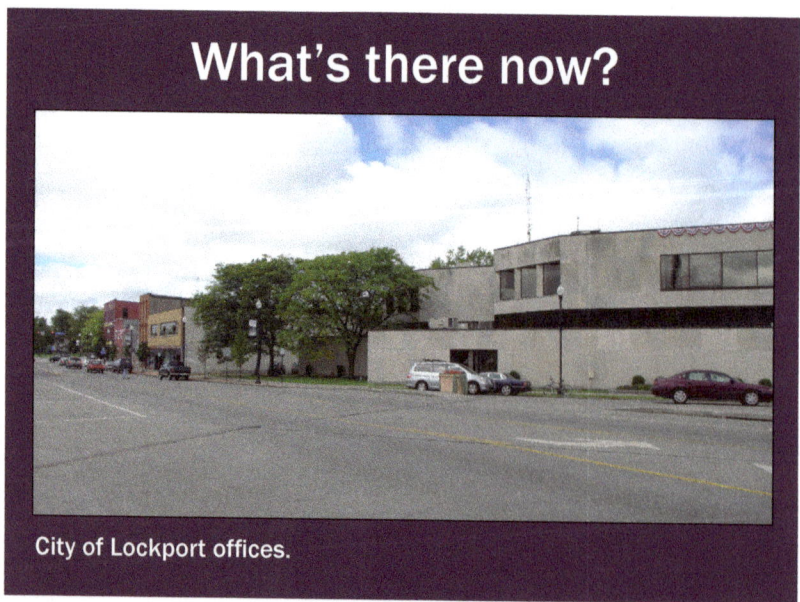
City of Lockport offices.

Poorhouses of the German Settlements Wheatfield, New York

The first German settlement was built on the Tonawanda Creek section of the Erie Canal. Each German village had its own church, and village society revolved around it.

St. Martini Lutheran Church was erected in Martinsville, a hamlet of Wheatfield, in 1846. The congregation then built a school and a poorhouse nearby. A fund was also set up to support widows and other poor members along with a Potter's Field burial plot for the poor.

St. Paul Lutheran Church, two blocks away in Martinsville, was founded in 1861. St. Martini's school and poorhouse property were transferred to St. Paul Lutheran Church in 1867. This poorhouse is recorded on an 1860 map but is not found in any records or on maps after 1875.

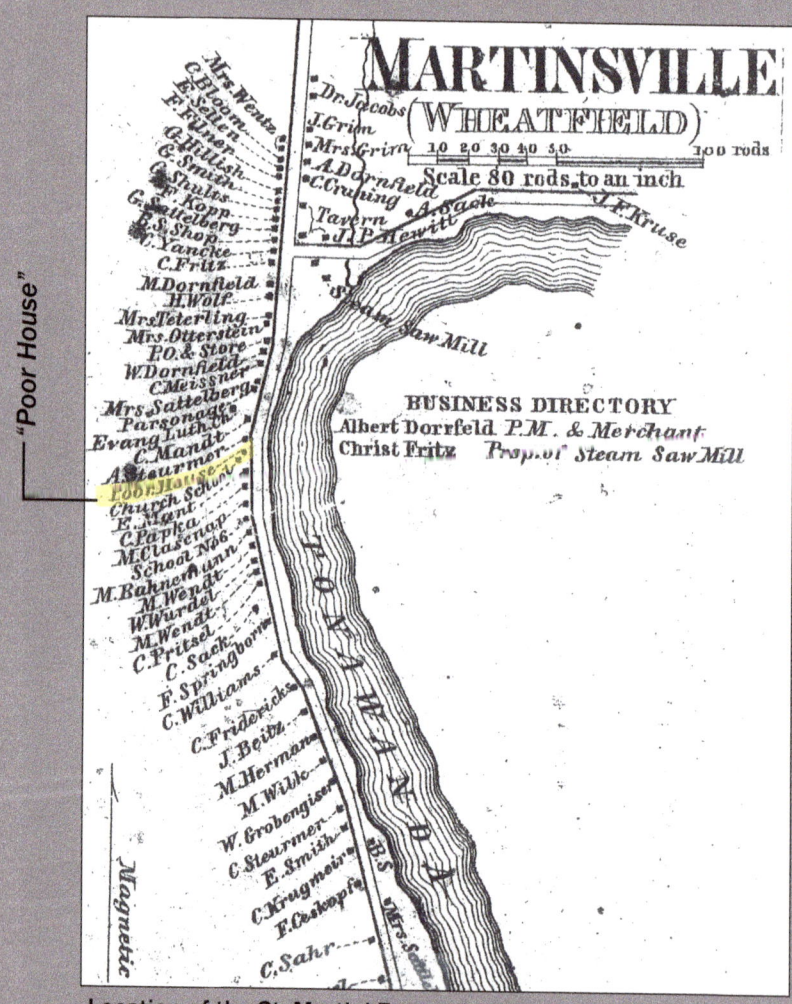

Location of the St. Martini Evangelical Lutheran Church "Poor House," 1860, Martinsville (Wheatfield).

> **There were two portable grave markers at one time on Potter's Field. One was a wooden cross that was moved here and there and the other, a moveable stone marker that read, 'To my friend' or something along that line.**
>
> **In reading the church history, I feel that any indigent in Martinsville was welcome to stay at the residence."**
>
> *Velma Camann, church historian, St. Paul's Church, 2010*

Bergholz: Holy Ghost Church

The first allowance made specifically for caring for the German poor in Bergholz came with the purchase of an additional 600 acres of land in 1843 by the trustees of the Bergholz congregation. This plot was set aside for the poorer families of this congregation. Located along Ward Road several miles from the main settlement site in Bergholz, the settlement was called Little Bergholz, later named St. Johnsburg in 1853.

"Witwe Haus" (Widows House), 1854, Bergholz

A private Witwe House was established in 1854 by Holy Ghost Church to care for its widows and children who had no support. Church members provided meals and the widows worked when possible. Capacity was six, plus children. A house was not needed for widowed husbands as they were likely to re-marry. The Widow's House was located on church property at Luther and Washington Streets in Bergholz.

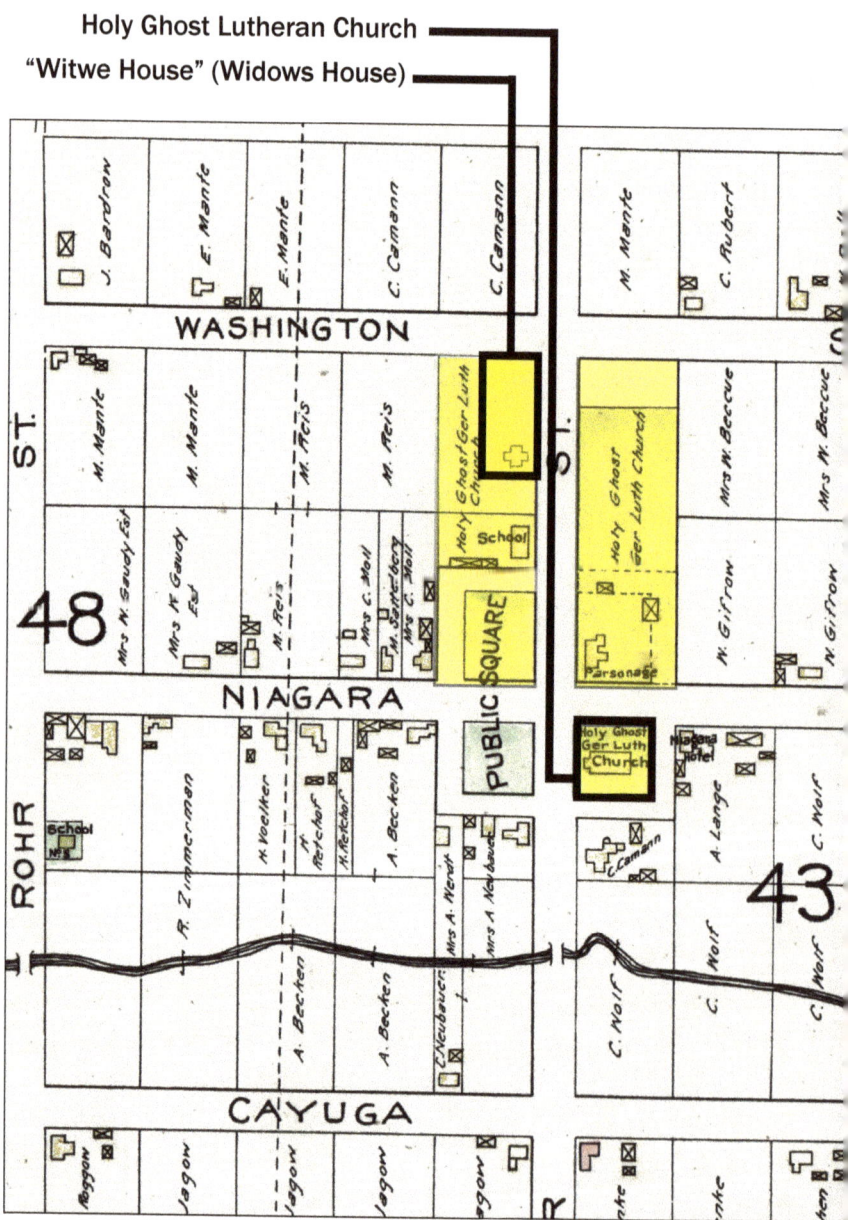

Holy Ghost Lutheran Church, Widows House, and church cemetery locations, Bergholz, Niagara County, 1908.

1808-1860   45

Holy Ghost Church Cemetery

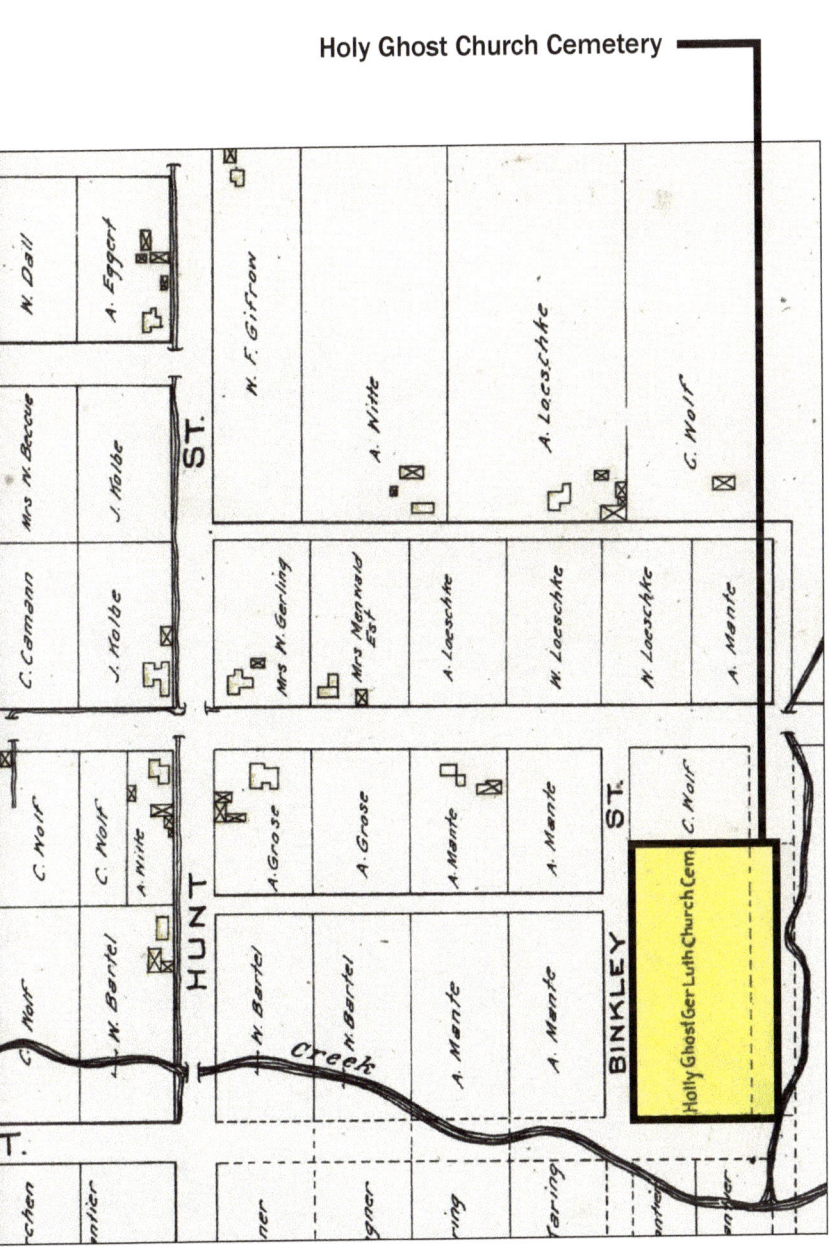

A private residence stands on the Martinsville poorhouse site today at 294 Old Falls Boulevard, North Tonawanda.

What's there now?

The German Heritage Museum at 2549 Niagara Road in Wheatfield, New York. "Das Haus" has information on German settlements in Niagara County.

Pest Houses of Niagara County

Pest houses were early, hospital-like facilities where sick people were quarantined. They were heavily used during plagues and epidemics to house those with communicable diseases such as smallpox, influenza, or tuberculosis.[4]

Many towns and cities had pest houses situated near poorhouses and usually near cemeteries. Pest houses are difficult to find because they were associated with epidemics and usually hidden away on the edges of growing towns and unlikely to show up in historical records. There are reports of temporary pest houses located in private homes, boarding houses, or outbuildings where disease outbreaks may have occurred.[5,6]

By the late 1880s, as medical knowledge about communicable diseases progressed, pest houses became known as quarantine hospitals, although citizens of the area and some official reports still referred to the facilities as pest houses.

The Pest House Medical Museum at the Old City Cemetery in Lynchburg, Virginia, is one of the few pest house museums in the country. Its exhibits replicate conditions and artifacts based upon historical records of early pest houses.

Pest House

An early, hospital-like place where sick people were quarantined during a plague or disease outbreak to house those afflicted with communicable diseases such as cholera, smallpox, and tuberculosis, or a shelter or hospital for those infected with a pestilential or contagious disease.

How to find pest house locations
- Look for older or relocated cemeteries in an area.
- Look for poorhouses (almshouses), which frequently had pest houses or isolation rooms.
- Look for "pest house" or "quarantine hospital" on old maps.
- Search records for pest house, quarantine hospital, disease, epidemic, plague (cholera, influenza, small pox).
- Look for major early construction projects worked by immigrants who lived in crowded, unsanitary conditions.

Niagara County Pest House on Almshouse Grounds 1852–1915

The Niagara County pest house was located on Niagara Street Extension at Gothic Hill Road in the Town of Lockport and was on the grounds of the Niagara County poorhouse. It was open until 1915. The pest house was located across the road from the poorhouse, where the Niagara County Jail is currently located.

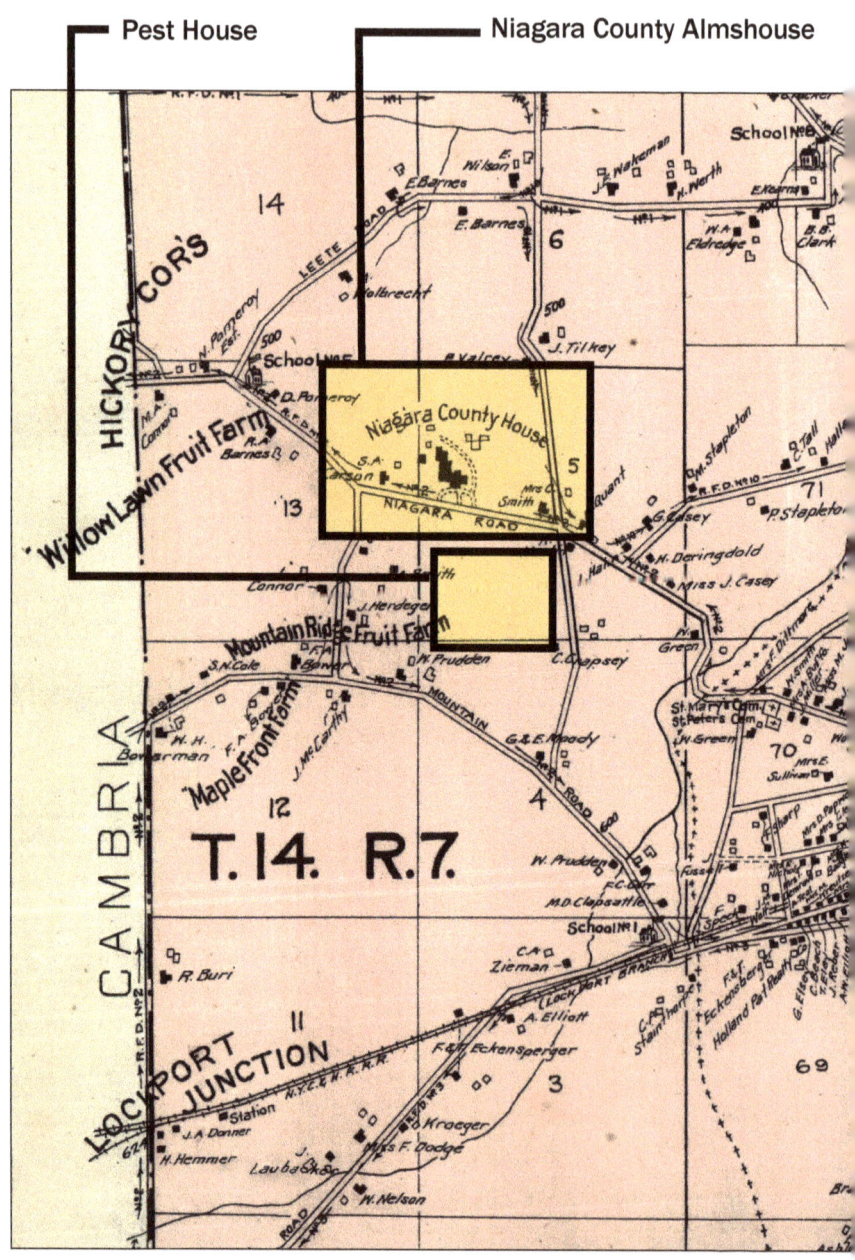

Niagara County Almshouse and pest house locations, Town of Lockport, 1908.

1808-1860 53

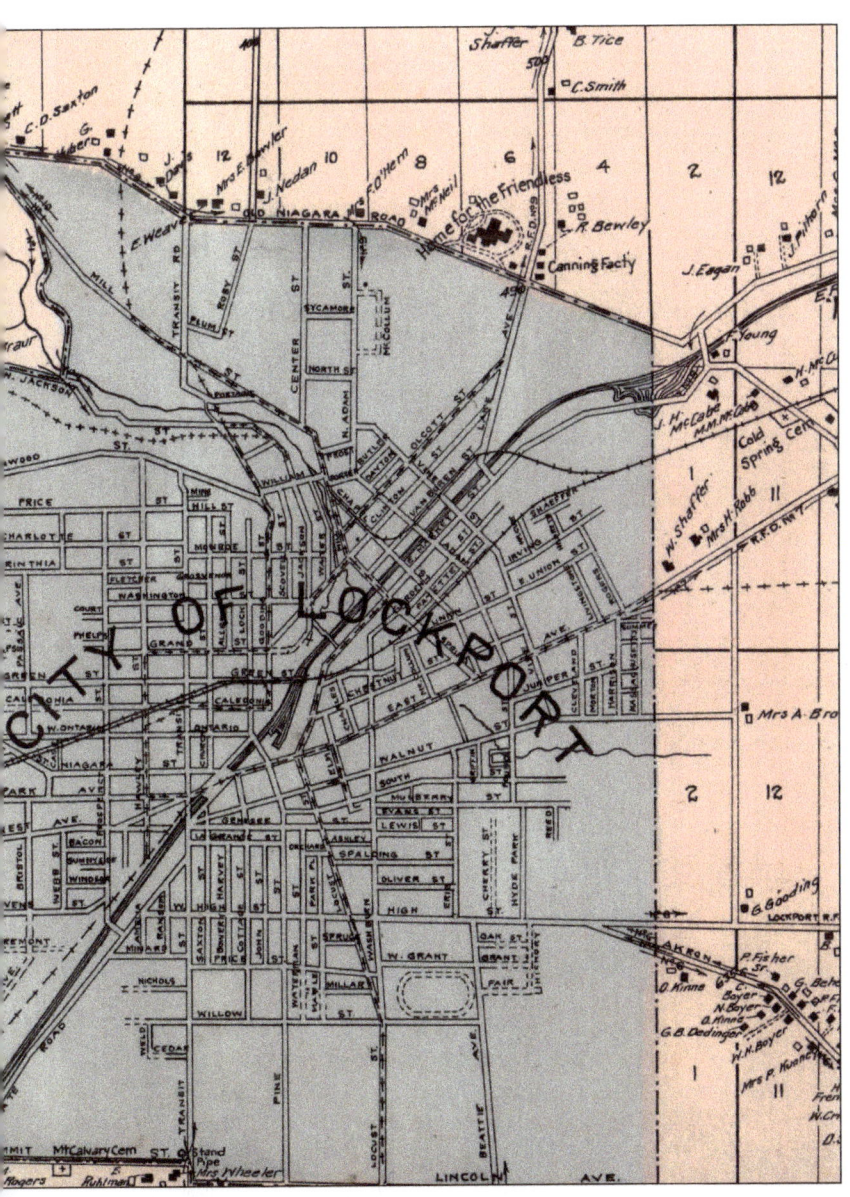

> For other infectious cases, the Superintendent has put up a small one-story cottage, and intends to erect another, and there is a small house which could be used as a pest-house on another part of the farm. There is another small wooden structure, intended for a dead-house."

Report from the New York State Charities Aid Association, 1886.

The Niagara County Pest House was described as a "small, one-story building, 14 x 24 feet, 9 feet tall with 18 inch thick stone walls," located on the south side of Niagara Street Extension. *Sketch by David J. LoTempio.*

There are reports that the pest house cemetery was located on the pest house grounds.[7,8] The pest house and poorhouse buildings located on the Niagara Street Extension at Gothic Hill have since been demolished, though remnants of the old poorhouse cemetery can still be found at the site today. See "Niagara County Almshouse" section for more information.

> **NIAGARA COUNTY POOR-HOUSE.**
>
> For contagious diseases, "there is a pest-house, situated about one hundred rods from the main building, used for small-pox cases;" and for lying-in women, "there are separate and convenient rooms;" but "there is no separate ward for surgical cases." For purifying the clothing of recent inmates, the "bath-rooms and disinfectants are freely used."
>
> The attending physician receives an annual salary of $350, the medicine being supplied by the county. A separate diet kitchen is maintained for the sick, and "they get what their cases require." There is "one male nurse at $2 per week;" the other nurses are paupers de-tailed for the purpose. No record of the sick is kept. The number of deaths during the year ending June 30, 1881, was sixteen, from diseases given as follows: "Gun-shot wound, one; stab in neck and lungs, one; consumption, three; dropsy, two; old age, one; softening of the brain, one; chronic inflammation of the bladder, one; heart disease, two; small-pox, one; senile gangrene, one; marasmus, one." The physician reports that "there were not over eight taking any drugs," July 1, 1881, and adds, "most of the patients have chronic diseases, — rheumatism, lung troubles, chronic ulcers; — but few fevers or acute attacks." The number of births reported in the house during the year was ten.

Excerpt from the *15th Annual Report of the State Board of Charities* (State of New York), **1882.**

For a description of the diseases mentioned in this chapter, see the definition section on page 301.

> **Dead House**
> A dead house or deadhouse is a building used for the temporary storage of a human corpse before burial or transportation.

Earth Yields 9 Skeletons at Jail Site

Human bone fragments, including several skulls and a lower jaw with one tooth intact, were unearthed about 11:30 Wednesday morning at the site of the new County Jail on Niagara St. Ext.

Pieces of at least nine skeletons were uncovered by an earthmover just east of the nearby completed building.

Records dating to 1852 fail to show a cemetery at the site, according to County Historian Clarence O. Lewis. But, he added, the position of the bones together with bits of wood and square-headed nails also uncovered would indicate that it was a private burial plot.

Earthmover operator Donald Mills, of Fillmore, a resident of DeFlippo's Hotel, 326 West, Ave., uncovered the first skull.

The sharp-eyed worker noticed that the blade of his machine "shaved the top of a skull off and left a hole in the ground," he told the Union-Sun & Journal. "At first I thought it was a prehistoric egg."

On later passes over the ground, he said, "we uncovered lots of bones. They formed a pattern—they were all laid side-by-side."

Mr. Mills said the B&M Earthmovers of Hamburg, his employer, had lowered the ground level about three feet before the bones turned up, and that another contractor had previously graded the site.

From the Lockport *Union-Sun and Journal*, September 1, 1960.

"UNEARTHED - Earthmover operator Donald Mills holds a skull and jawbone that were among the skeleton fragments uncovered by the giant machines at the site of the new County Jail Wednesday."[9] September 1, 1960, Lockport *Union-Sun and Journal*.

> I was puzzled as to why the pest house and burials were on the south side of the road instead of on the County Poor House farm across the way. Perhaps it was a village pest house rather than one for county patients. So I spent two days going through old village records with no results. I had then to conclude that it must have been a county Pest House and that county paupers having smallpox or cholera were isolated there and that burials of victims were close by. The regular Poor House Cemetery was a considerable distance north of the road, and of the Poor House itself."

Clarence O. Lewis, Thursday, Sept. 22, 1960, Lockport Union-Sun and Journal

What's there now?

Reports about the pest house indicate the structure was on the south side of the property on the present site of the Niagara County Jail.

Pest Houses of Niagara Falls

Pest houses and quarantine hospitals are not well-documented places of care. Two Niagara Falls pest houses are good examples of abandoned history. The only evidence of their existence is found in a few local newspaper accounts. Both of these older houses were located near Oakwood Cemetery. Historical records are not clear as to their dates of operation.

In the nineteenth century, Niagara Falls residents who contracted contagious diseases such as cholera, tuberculosis, and smallpox were quarantined in the pest house. Most patients died because medical care was primitive. Oakwood Cemetery was nearby for burial. *Sketch by David J. LoTempio.*

The old pest house – A newspaper reference from 1893.

> It was learned on reliable authority that the pest house when established by the old town of the Falls, was located in the neighborhood of where 15th Street will be. The present pest house is about on a line of the extension of 12th street and is therefore nearer the city by seven hundred feet.

Niagara Falls Gazette, October 23, 1893.

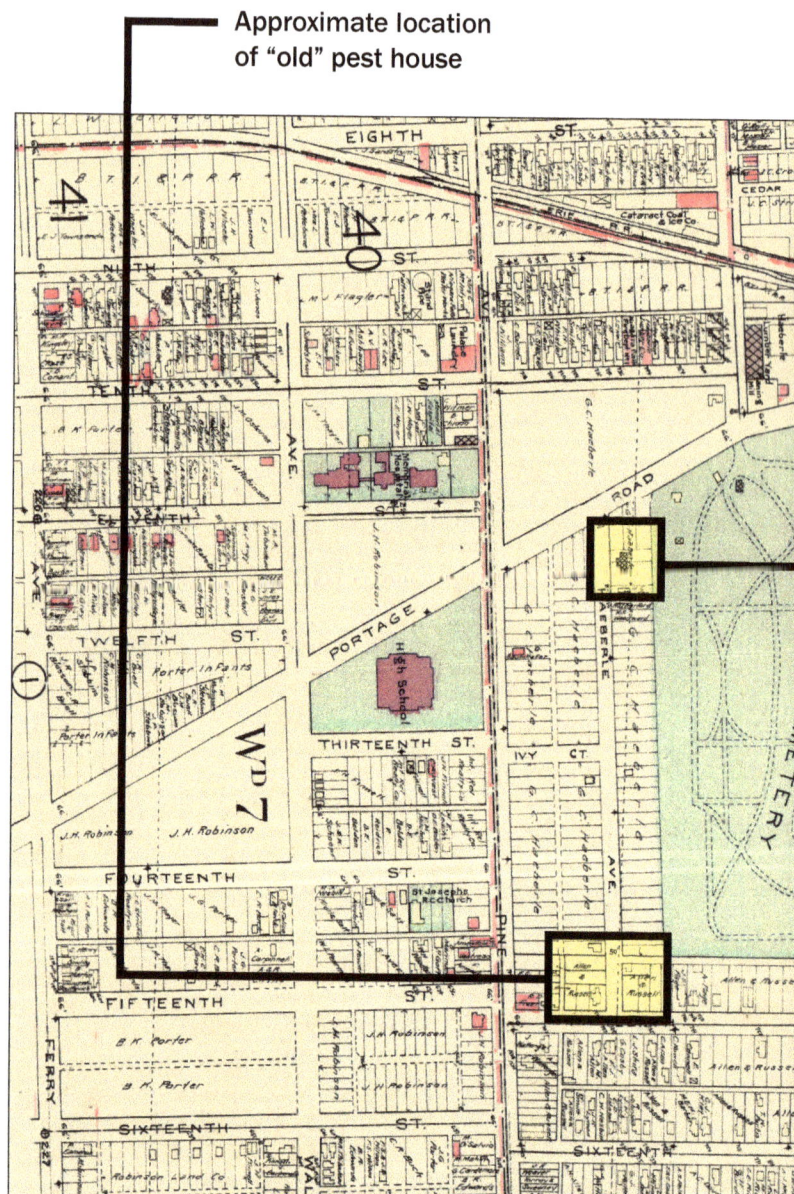

Pest house locations, Niagara Falls.

1808-1860   61

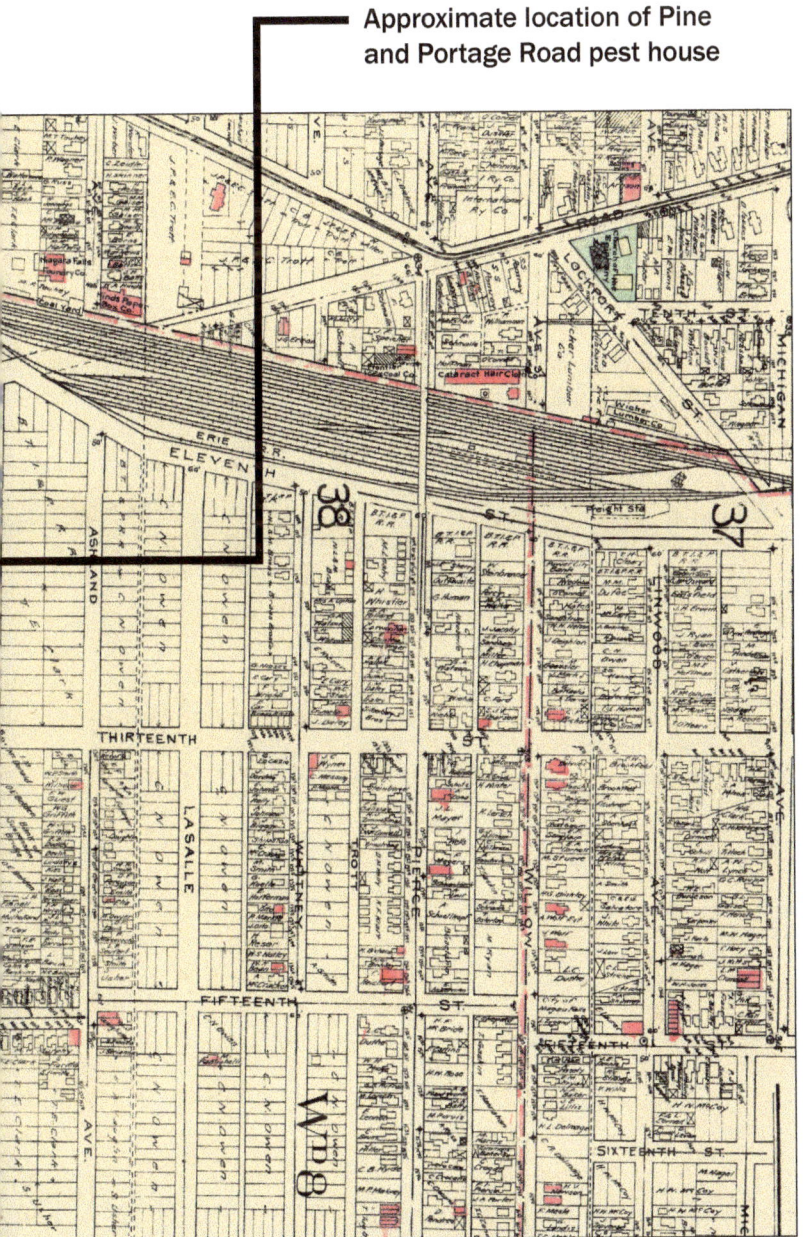

Approximate location of Pine and Portage Road pest house

People of Tenth Street Indignant over the Pest House Nuisance which Has Been Saddled on Them

The long and short of the matter is this. The city was compelled to supply a pest house. The matter was discussed in the Common Council and the mayor appointed a committee composed of Messrs. Maloney, Earles and Noblett to arrange for the construction of the house. Alterman Strickler took considerable interest in this matter and on June 6th last he was substituted as chairman of the committee in place of Alderman Maloney. It was generally understood that the house was to be erected near the center of the lot up near the cemetery fence so that if any deaths occurred from Cholera, small pox or other malignant and dangerous diseases, the remains could be taken into the cemetery and interred without bringing them out on the public road. Instead of this plan being carried out the residents of Tenth Street claim that the pest house has been erected within 500 feet of the front doors of their residences and but 100 feet from the Portage road.

Niagara Falls Gazette, October 23, 1893.

What's there now?

Oakwood Cemetery, Niagara Falls. Two of the town's early pest houses were located along the cemetery fence.

DeVeaux School for Orphan and Destitute Children
1857–1971

Upon his death in 1852, Judge Samuel DeVeaux bequeathed to the Protestant Episcopal Church, under the Diocese of Western New York, sixty acres of land and $154,352 for the establishment of a school. The DeVeaux School for Orphan and Destitute Children was located at 2900 Lewiston Road in Niagara Falls and later became known as DeVeaux College.

The DeVeaux School was created for the free education of worthy boys who had lost one or both parents. Judge DeVeaux left funds for the school because he was grateful for his own good fortune, crediting his parents for ensuring his proper education.

> **Destitute**
> Without means of subsistence, lacking food, clothing, and shelter; completely impoverished. Very poor.

Top: DeVeaux School seal. Bottom: DeVeaux School for Orphan and Destitute Children, 2900 Lewiston Road, Niagara Falls.

DeVeaux School underwent several transformations from its original concept. First a school for orphans, it then became a private school for orphans and private-pay students. It was a military school until 1950 and finally closed in 1971. In 1972 it reopened as a school for children with learning disabilities. In 1978 it was purchased by Niagara University. In 2000 the State of New York acquired DeVeaux Campus, making it the 159th state park. DeVeaux Woods State Park is a fifty-acre parcel of land along the Niagara Gorge escarpment, off the Robert Moses Parkway between Whirlpool Park and Devils Hole Park, North Main Street (Lewiston Road), Niagara Falls.

Laying the Cornerstone for Schoellkopf Hall, the new dormitory for boys, DeVeaux School, November 3, 1929. Left to right: Reverend Dr. William S. Barrows, Headmaster; Reverend Doctor Cameron Davis, Class of 1890; Mr. Paul Schoellkopf, who donated $50,000 for construction of the building; Paul Schoellkopf, Jr., his son; unidentified man; and Rt. Reverend Frederick L. Deans, a bishop from Scotland.

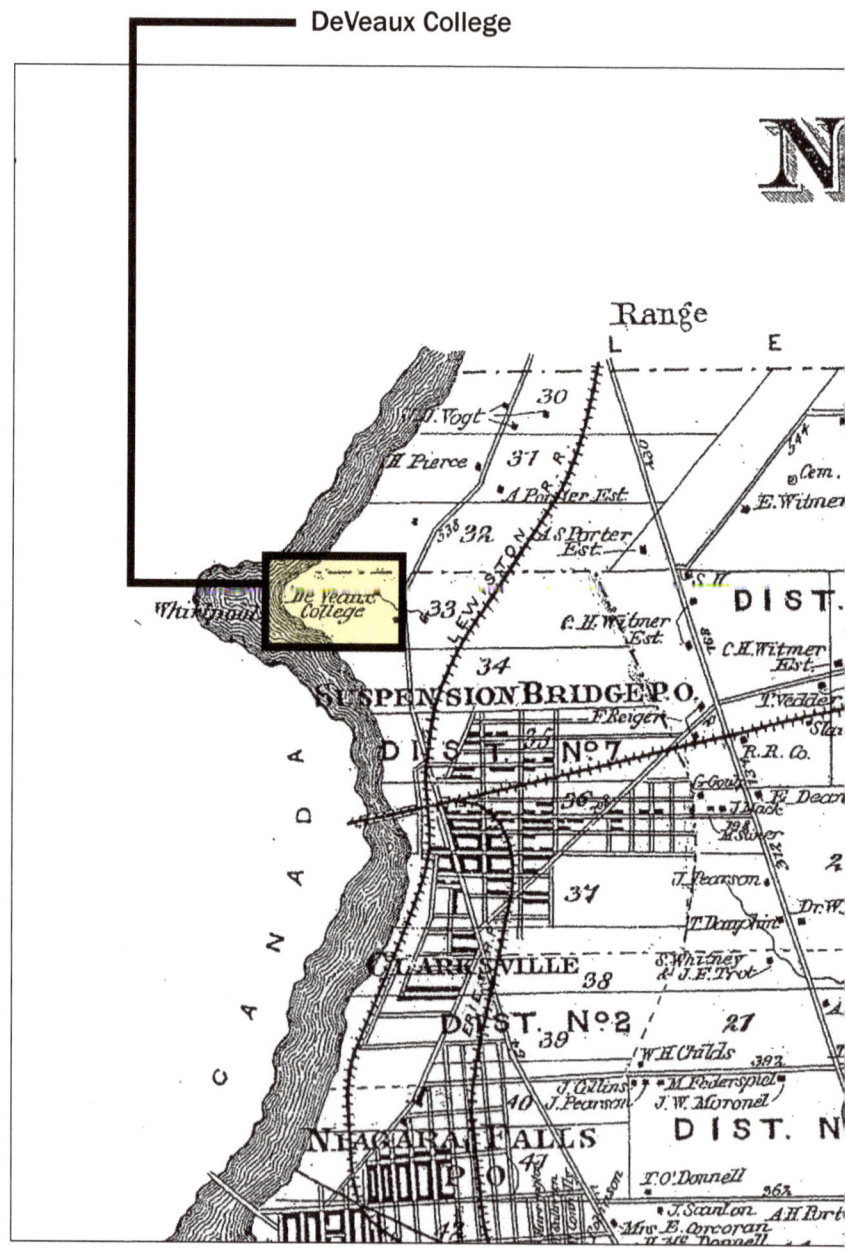

DeVeaux College on an 1875 map of Niagara.

1808-1860   69

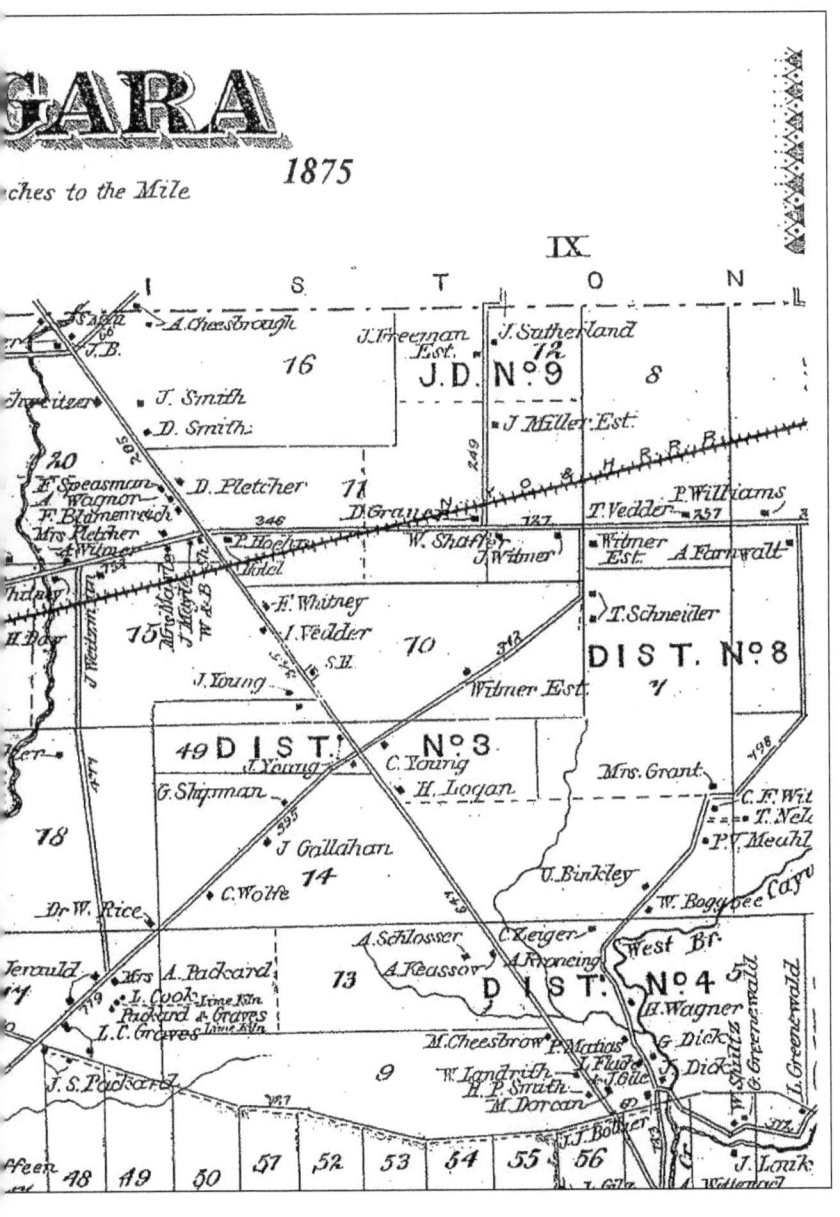

```
Will                    Exemplified Copy of Will
        or              Dated August 3 1852
Samuel DeVeaux          Probated in Niagara County,
                        November 13 1852
                        Recorded April 3 1856 in
                        Liber 173 of Deeds at page 354
                                Makes various bequests and
appoints William H. Delaney, William Shelton, Peter A. Porter and
Richard H. Woodruff, trustees to form an institution for the educa-
tion of orphan and destitute children, directs that his name be
attached to same and that said trustees convey to said institution
the remainder of his estate within five years after his decease.
```

A portion of the 1852 will of Samuel DeVeaux, outlining his wishes for the formation of "an institution for the education of orphan and destitute children."[10]

DeVeaux students and their geometry instructor, Mr. Mellen (center); 1st Lieutenant U. T. Page (far right), 2nd Lieutenant L. E. Birdsey (right), and 1st Sergeant M. G. Argus (far left). Dates on the board are 1865–1887.[11]

Aerial view of DeVeaux School campus, circa 1965.

Schoellkopf Hall, a dormitory, was built in 1929 and is the last remaining school building of DeVeaux College. The hall is now part of DeVeaux Woods State Park.

Monro Hall (1886), left, and Patterson Hall, right rear (1888), were both demolished in 1989.

Van Rensselaer Hall, the main school building, was built in 1855 and demolished in 1989.

1808-1860   73

Dedication plaque inside the entrance to Schoellkopf Hall.

DE VEAUX COLLEGE,

Suspension Bridge, N. Y.

DE VEAUX COLLEGE is beautifully situated on the Niagara River, two and a half miles below the Falls; the grounds reserved for its use embrace nearly one hundred acres. The College Edifice is spacious and commodious, well ventilated, warmed by steam, lighted with gas, with ample bathing facilities, and, in all particulars, equipped for health and comfort. By Grammar School courses of study boys are fitted for the Colleges and Universities; for the United States Military Academy, the Naval School, or business. The domestic organization is military. The College year begins Wednesday, September 2d. Charges, $400 per annum. Registers, with full details, will be sent on application.

The Rev. GEORGE HERBERT PATTERSON, at the renewed and urgent solicitation of the Trustees, and contrary to recent notice, will retain the Presidency of the College.

Advertisement for DeVeaux College, 1870s.

*§ 13. Whenever application for admission into the De Veaux college for orphan and destitute children shall be made by or for an orphan and destitute child, under the provisions of the will of Samuel De Veaux, deceased, and of the act incorporating said college, said orphan and destitute child, with the consent of the persons or officers hereinafter mentioned, may, of his own free will, bind himself by indenture to said corporation, to be admitted into said college as an orphan and destitute child, to be there maintained and educated according to the provisions, and in the manner and under all the regulations and restraints, directed or contained in the said will, or as the said corporation shall, from time to time, make under said will, or under the act hereby amended, or such amendments as may, from time to time, be made thereto, and such binding shall be as valid and effectual as if such infant was of full age at the time of such engagement. § 1, ch. 385, 1857.

Excerpt taken from the *Poor Laws of the State of New York*, 1871.

What's there now?

Interior of Schoellkopf Hall.

School for Colored Deaf, Dumb, and Blind Children, Niagara City, Suspension Bridge, New York (now Niagara Falls) 1857–1860

A controversial pioneer of education, Dr. Platt H. Skinner, a Prattsburg, New York, native, ran a remarkable school for African-American children who had multiple disabilities.

The School for the Instruction of Colored Deaf, Dumb, and Blind Children was located in the hamlet of Suspension Bridge, New York, now known as Niagara Falls.

Dr. Skinner, a deeply religious white man with progressive blindness, and his young wife who was hearing impaired, arrived in 1858 in Suspension Bridge. They were seeking a location where he would establish his second boarding school for African-American children who were disabled.

The Skinners journeyed north to Niagara after a mysterious fire at his first school in Washington, D.C. In Washington., Dr. Skinner was accused of neglect and was forced to leave his school.

Platt Henry Skinner

A train crosses on the upper level of the famous Suspension Bridge. Foot and horse traffic crossed on the lower level. The bridge was the only railway route to Canada.

Because he was an outspoken abolitionist and fought for racial equality, it is believed the charges against him may be false. Students from Dr. Skinner's Washington school would became the nucleus of Gallaudet University, a famous institution for the education of the deaf.

Dr. Skinner was educated at Oberlin College in Ohio.[12] According to Oberlin College records, he was enrolled in the Preparatory Department from 1843 to 1846. He then trained as a dentist and practiced dentistry in New York City from 1851 to 1855. Dr. Skinner worked in the notorious Five Points section of New York City with poor children and their families during the 1850s. He produced two booklets that called attention to their poverty and horrid conditions. In 1852 he published "The Voice of the Young" on behalf of Temperance, Truth, and Safety, and

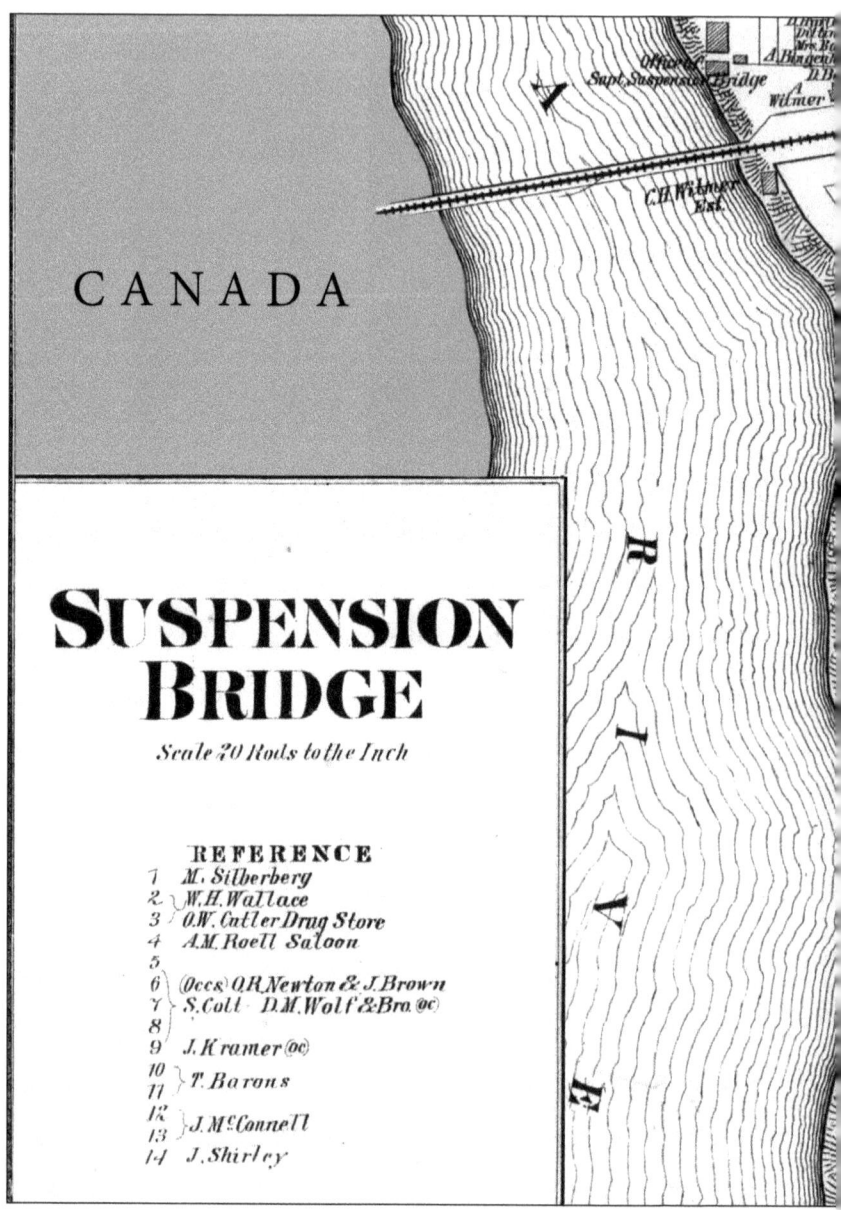

The highlighted block on this 1875 map indicates the approximate location of the school at 26 Lewiston Road as it would have been in 1858. Suspension Bridge is now part of modern Niagara Falls.

1808-1860 81

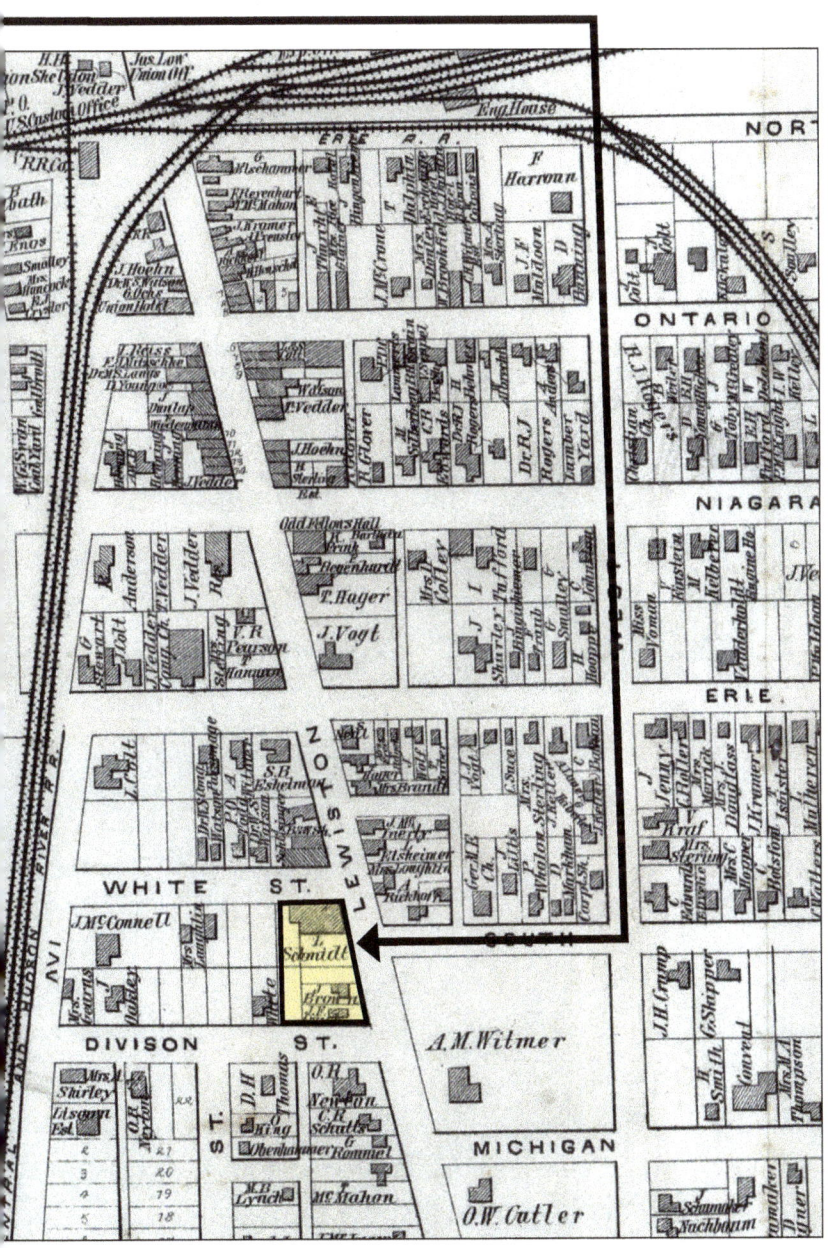

in 1854, "The Little Ragged Ten Thousand, Scenes of Actual Life Among the Lowly."[13]

A *New York Times* announcement in 1854 mentioned that Platt H. Skinner and Jerusha M. Hills were married by the Rev. Thomas Gallaudet, a well known advocate for the deaf.[14]

From all accounts, Dr. Skinner's school was a happy and productive place. Students learned to communicate through sign language. They were encouraged to help each other and to complement each other's abilities. "We must teach the hand of the mute to perform the office of the tongue, and the eye to perform the office of the ear; the fingers of the blind must be taught to see," Dr. Skinner wrote in an 1858 report.

A visitor to the school, Mrs. Julia Watson, provides an early description:

> At the Suspension Bridge we found an Asylum for the deaf, dumb, and blind. It was a private school kept by Dr. Skinner and his wife. The Doctor had been blind two years—his wife, though she could see, was a mute. This worthy couple, though white themselves, were deeply interested in the poor colored children afflicted like themselves, and their pupils are all colored. Those who could see had bright

Dr. Skinner published a newspaper, *The Mute and the Blind*, from 1859 through the mid-1860s. Copies of some issues are available for research at the Old Sturbridge Village Research Library, Sturbridge, Massachusetts, and the Museum of disABILITY, Buffalo, New York.

sparkling eyes, were quiet and respectful. The blind were very tidy and attentive. They all seemed very contented and happy, and it was interesting to see the dumb scholars converse with their blind associates.

The institution is supported partly by donations and contributions from those who sympathize in the good work, and partly by the publication of the paper– the work is done by the pupils who are printers and compositors.

We came away much pleased with our visit and praying for the success and prosperity of the Asylum, and for the welfare of the generous instructors and founders.[15]

A view of the lower roadway of the Suspension Bridge from the American side facing Canada. The large sign above the two men sitting on the right indicates there was a concern that people marching across might cause the bridge to sway. This concern was so great that the fine was a small fortune in those days: "A fine of $50 to $100 will be imposed for marching over the bridge."

The United States Census of 1860 records the residents of Dr. Skinner's school. At that time Dr. Skinner was listed as a thirty-year-old blind male. Other residents listed included his wife, four-year-old son, students, and a printer.

In addition to running the school, Dr. Skinner published a newspaper, *The Mute and the Blind.* The paper was sold in the local community and sent to supporters of the school by mail. It was also used as a vehicle for raising funds and as a training tool for the students. "We find by experience that, a blind boy can run our press with about as much speed, as a man who has his sight, and can perform equally as good labor," Dr. Skinner wrote in one article. "Thus, our press is now run: A blind boy at the helm; a deaf-mute girl to arrange the sheets, and a deaf-mute roller."

Finding the funds to keep the school going was a constant struggle for Dr. Skinner and his wife. His various writings in the newspaper and reports are filled with appeals for financial support. The school had nine students in 1858 and Dr. Skinner hoped to increase the number to twenty by the next year, but only if the means could be found. "We are engaged in teaching a class of the most despised and unfortunate creatures in the world. We need help to carry on this work," he wrote in one issue of his newspaper. "My brother, shall these poor children be shut out from the sympathies of your heart," he implored in the flowery language typical of those times. "I trust not."

The school's location was probably not a coincidence, given Dr. Skinner's passionate abolitionist views. The bridge offered an easy passage to Canada and freedom for fugitive slaves. Both the top train and track and the lower roadway were used in the Underground Railroad. The lower deck was opened in 1854, with Canada only 825 feet away. The proximity of the bridge, in fact, may have been a primary factor in the selection of the Niagara site.

The border between the United States and Canada had become vitally important after Congress passed the Fugitive Slave Act of 1850. That controversial law required states to arrest and return fugitive slaves, so for many, Canada was the only option for freedom.

Dr. Skinner discussed the location of the school in an 1858 report:

The Underground Railroad

Slaves and the people who helped them to escape used Railroad terms to code their activities:

LINE.....................a route from safe house to safe house

STATION................a safe house where fleeing slaves could hide

STOCKHOLDERS......providers of food and clothing for fugitive slaves

CONDUCTORS........people who helped transport slaves from station to station

One of the more well-known conductors on the Underground Railroad was Harriet Tubman who led many escapees across the Suspension Bridge to safety on the other side of the Niagara River in Canada. By 1858, when Dr. Skinner located his school in the village of Suspension Bridge, there were several communities of fugitive slaves established nearby in Canada. Historians are unsure, but there is reason to believe that Dr. Skinner himself was a conductor on the Underground Railroad.

The buildings above are located on the site of the school today at 1810 Main Street (formerly Lewiston Avenue) in Niagara Falls. In 1858 the school was located above a grocery store at 26 Lewiston Avenue, Suspension Bridge. The center building above is roughly at the same location as Dr. Skinner's school.[16]

The question of locality is one of vital importance to such a school. On the one hand, we have pupils from Canada, whose friends are exceedingly tenacious about their children going far toward the borders of what seems to them a most horrid pit-hole – I mean the borders of slavery. On the other hand, we have pupils from the southern States, whose friends complain that it is too far north where we now are; they urge that their children cannot endure the extreme cold of the climate. Such an institution should be located so as to accommodate the largest number of those who are likely to need its benefits. Such a question as this cannot be decided in a day.

Noted African-American historian Michael Boston, PhD, describes Skinner's choices against the backdrop of racial tensions that shaped others' views of him:

Furthermore, in regard to slavery, Skinner was an abolitionist and activist. He boldly let his views be known, orally and in print, whether he was in Washington, Suspension Bridge or Trenton. Being a promoter of equality for all racial groups, he supported the anti-slavery activities of others and may have even been a conductor on the Underground Railroad. Consequently, the controversial abolitionist educator, Dr. P. H. Skinner, was definitely an enigma; although at times he was misunderstood, his personality made him either friends or enemies at a volatile time in United States history.[17]

During the time immediately preceding the Civil War, Dr. Skinner and his school became a victim of growing public pressure in Niagara Falls. When the pressure became too intense, he and his wife moved the school to its third and final location in Trenton, New Jersey. Dr. Skinner died in 1866. Shortly after his death, the Trenton School was intentionally burned.

The following excerpt from a letter addressed to the Volta Bureau (founded by Alexander Graham Bell for "the increase and diffusion of knowledge relating to the Deaf") gives a good overview of the life of Dr. Platt H. Skinner.

July 29, 1914

When I was examining the history of Mr. Skinner's labor on behalf of the Deaf I came to the conclusion that the "systematic efforts which had been made to blacken his character" arose from the fact that his sympathies had been aroused on behalf of the colored Deaf and Dumb and Blind at a time when Slavery existed in the United States, and the color line was sharply drawn. In looking over the records of the trial which resulted in the transference of Skinner's pupils to the care of Amos Kendall and the establishment of the Columbia Institute for the Deaf and Dumb at Kendall Green, I can read very readily between the lines that Mr. Skinner had profoundly outraged the feelings of the community at Washington by receiving a colored lad into his school along with Whites. The race question was a burning issue in those days and prejudices were easily aroused. That Mr. Skinner, though probably of the militant type like John Brown, was essentially a philanthropic man is evidenced by his subsequent career. He went as close to the Canadian Boundary as he could get and opened a school exclusively for the colored Deaf and Dumb and Blind, and edited a paper some copies of which you have in the Bureau.

Alexander Graham Bell

Dr. Skinner's tombstone, located in Riverview Cemetery in Trenton, New Jersey. It reads: In Memory of Dr Platt Henry Skinner, A native of Prattsburgh, N.Y. Died Jan. 1, 1866 in Trenton, N.J. Aged 42 years and 10 months & 11 days. Here lies the friend and benefactor of the Colored Deaf and Dumb & Blind. "Blessed are they which are persecuted for rightousness' sake: for theirs is the kingdom of Heaven" St. Mathew 5:10

> Jan 1. - SKINNER, Dr. P.H., a blind man, editor of the magazine, *The Mute and the Blind* and the first instructor in this country of colored, blind and deaf mute children, for whose sakes he sacrificed all his property, died at Trenton, N.J.

Dr. Skinner's death on January 1, 1866, was among the deaths of prominent individuals reported in *Necrology of 1866* and published by *The New York Times* at the beginning 1867. Each year in January the *Times* published a list of deaths that had taken place during the previous year.

CHAPTER 2
1870s-1906

Home for the Friendless and Wyndham Lawn Home for Children
Lockport, New York
1871–Present

The Home for the Friendless movement started with the American Female Guardian Society, 24 Beekman Street, New York City, leading to the establishment of many Homes for the Friendless across the country. The newsletters of the American Female Guardian Society list donations, life memberships, and letters from Lockport area residents.

The Lockport Ladies Relief Society and the Home for the Friendless were organized in September 1865. The Ladies Relief Society in its early years collected and donated food and household items to needy families. Because of the number of children at the Niagara County poorhouse, a house for orphans, uncared for children, and elderly women was started in 1871.[1]

The first Home for the Friendless was in Lockport, located at 387 High Street, purchased for $5,000 from F. N. Nelson. The Ladies Relief Society raised $3,000, and the Board of Supervisors contributed about $3,500. Because of the growing need for the care of orphans, the first building used for the home was closed in 1892 and the organization moved to a larger facility.

The first Home for the Friendless, 1871–1892, was located at 387 High Street, Lockport.

Top and bottom photos: Interior of 387 High Street, Lockport.

96 Chapter 2

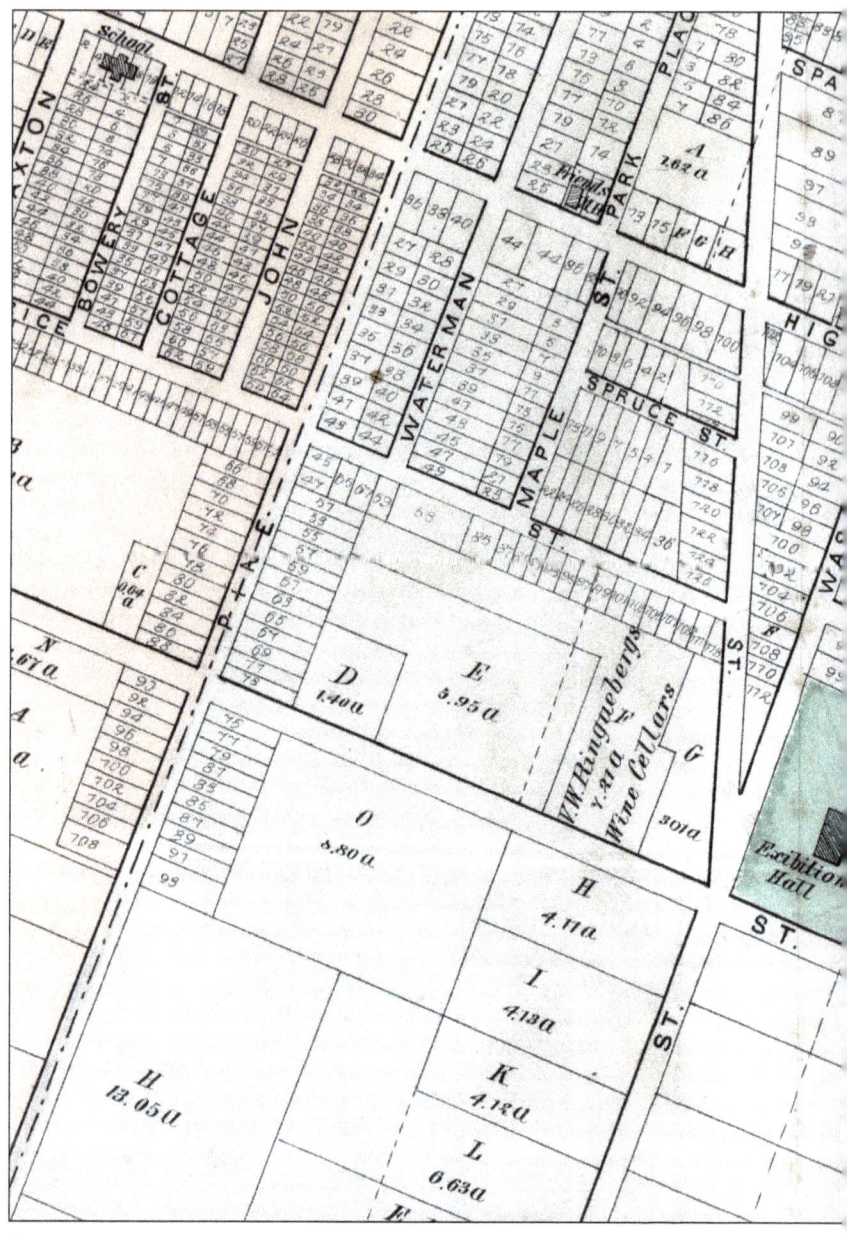

The Home for the Friendless, Niagara County, 1875.

1870s–1906   97

Home for the Friendless

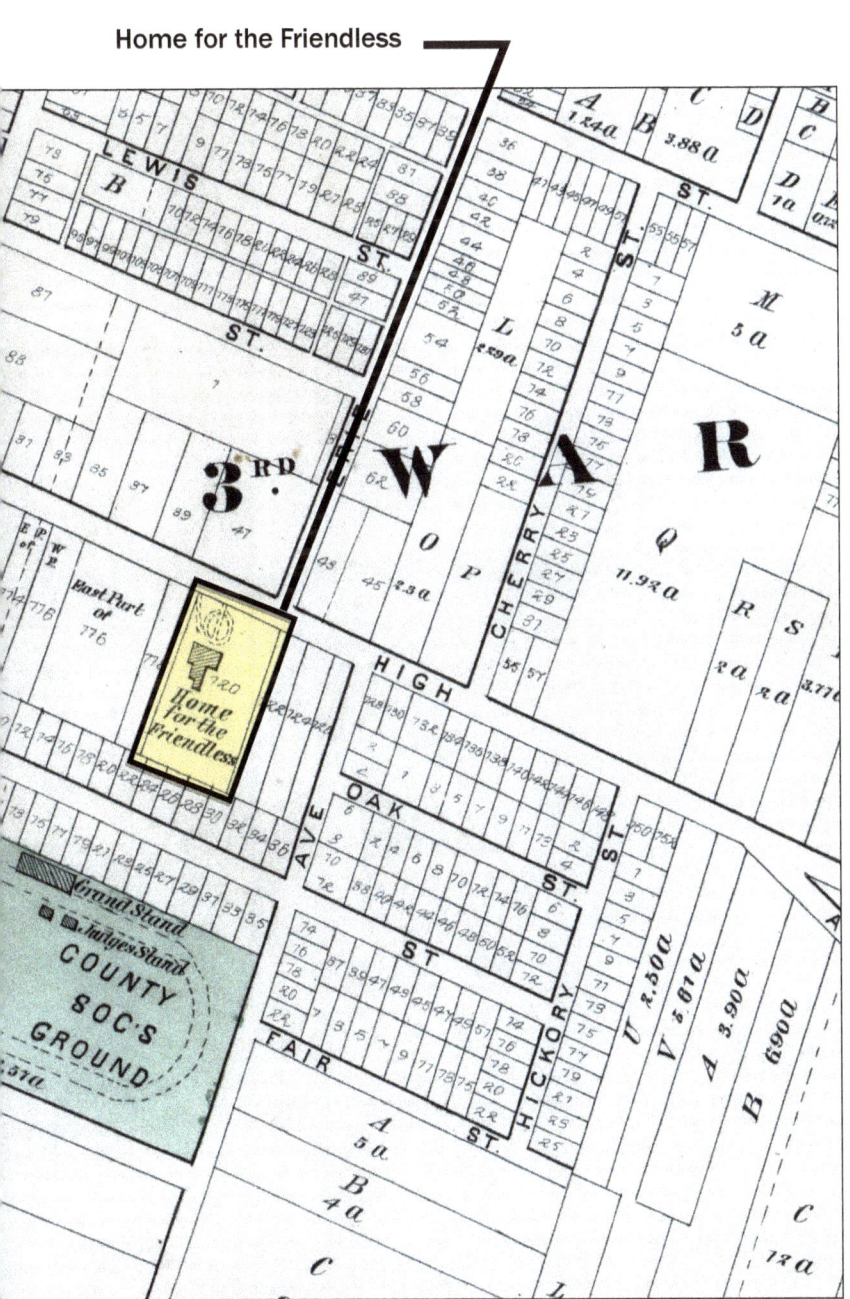

> In 1875 a State Law was passed forbidding County Poor Houses to retain children of pauper parents. The Lockport Home for the Friendless took as many of these children as their capacity permitted. Some two and a half acres of land had been purchased in connection with the house and altogether it was a good beginning for the Association...The first year 29 children and three old ladies were admitted to the Home."

Wyndham Lawn Home *by Clarence O. Lewis, 1931. From the files of the Niagara County Historian.*

What's there now?

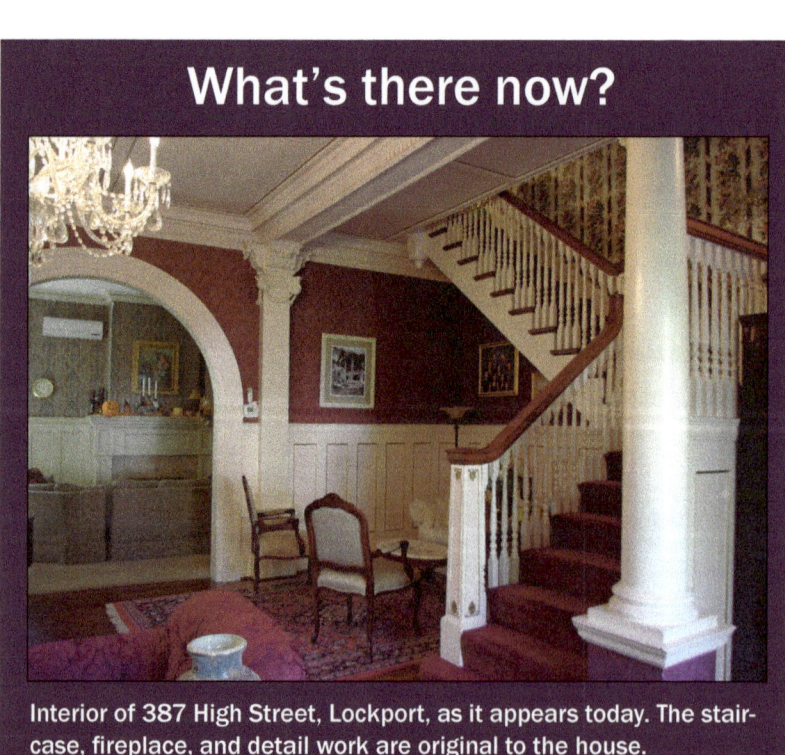

Interior of 387 High Street, Lockport, as it appears today. The staircase, fireplace, and detail work are original to the house.

Home for the Friendless (Wyndham Lawn), the new building, 1892–present

In 1892 the Home for the Friendless moved to a much larger estate formerly owned by Governor Washington Hunt. The Hunt Estate, located at 6395 Old Niagara Road in Lockport, was purchased from Mrs. Ella Hodge on May 14, 1892, for $30,000.[2] In 1901 the John Hodge Memorial Hospital was built on the grounds. The hospital was funded by Ella C. Hodge in honor of her late husband John Hodge to serve the medical needs of the resident children and staff.

In 1917 the Home for the Friendless was renamed Wyndham Lawn Home for Children. Wyndham Lawn ceased its function as an orphan home in 1972 but is used today as a home for children with emotional and behavioral difficulties. It is a residential facility operated by New Directions Youth and Family Services, with a capacity for forty-eight children and a private school.

The second location of the Home for the Friendless, at 6395 Old Niagara Road, Lockport.

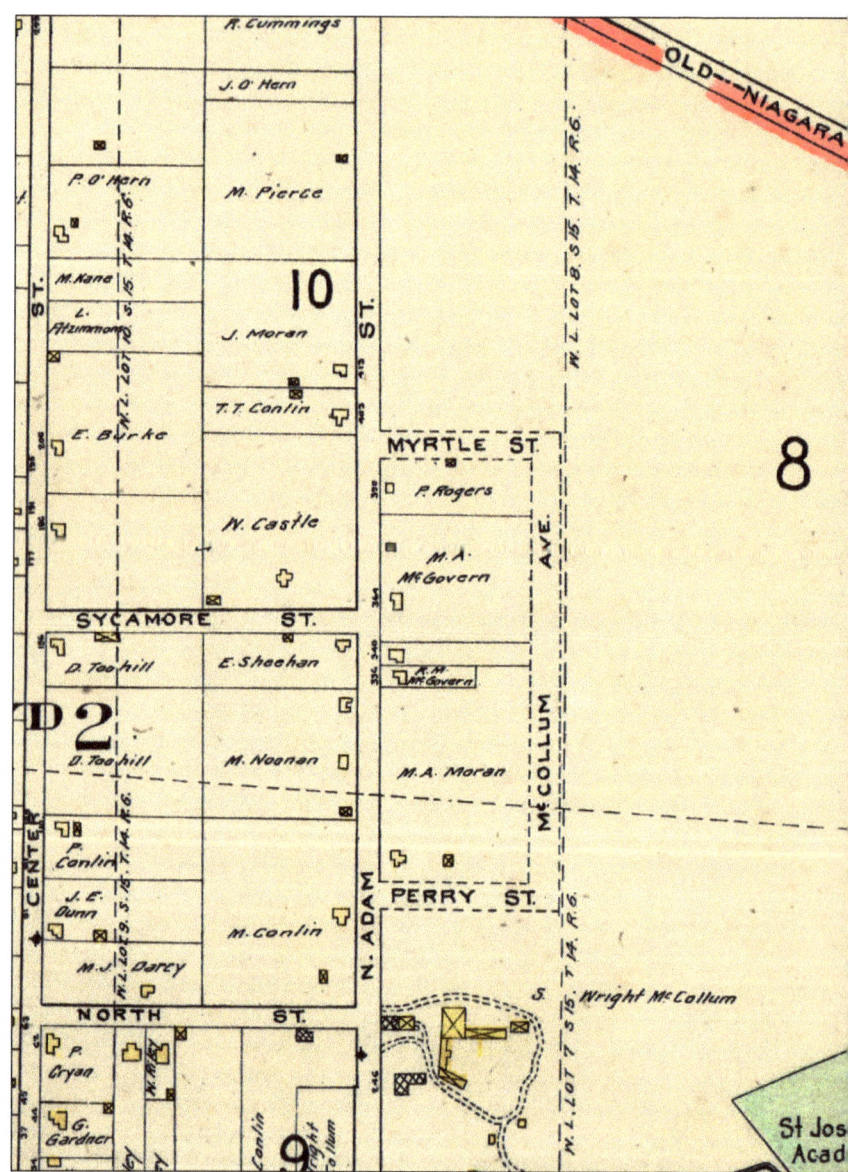

Home for the Friendless (Wyndham Lawn), Lake Avenue (Route 78) and Old Niagara Road, Lockport, 1908.

1870s-1906   101

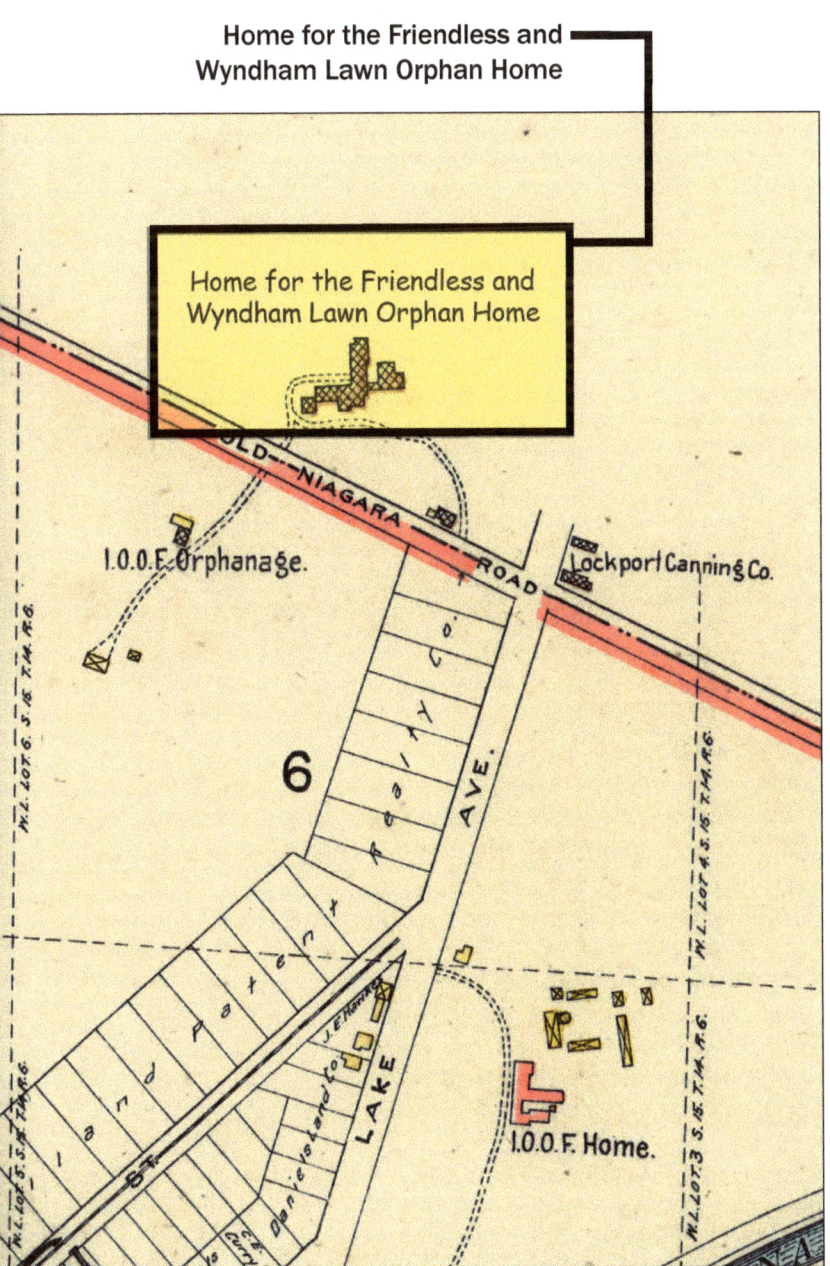

Niagara County—Private Charity.
HOMES FOR CHILDREN.

LOCKPORT HOME FOR THE FRIENDLESS (THE) ORPHAN,
Lake Avenue, Lockport, N. Y.

Inspected by Inspector Moxcey January 28, 1902; by Inspector Weeden December 14, 1901.

Established and incorporated February 8, 1871.

Objects.—To provide for the relief of orphan and friendless children and indigent women.

Governing body.—Board of Trustees.

President.—John E. Pound, Lockport.

Secretary.—Joseph A. Ward, Lockport.

Treasurer.—Charles J. Townsend, Lockport.

Attending physician.—C. A. Blackley, M. D.

Matron.—Miss Louise A. Ladd.

Value of property, $79,520.60.

Number of children cared for during the year, 113 (of whom 72 were supported by public funds and 41 by private funds); remaining October 1, 1902, 31 (14 boys and 17 girls).

Receipts for the year ending September 30, 1902, including balance on hand ($250.79), $9,942.44; expenditures, $9,015.04; balance on hand October 1, 1902, $927.40.

Qualifications for admittance.—Destitute children under 16 years of age are received free.

Application to be made to the president.

Excerpt taken from the 1902 New York State *Annual Report of the State Board of Charities*, Volume 36, Part 2.

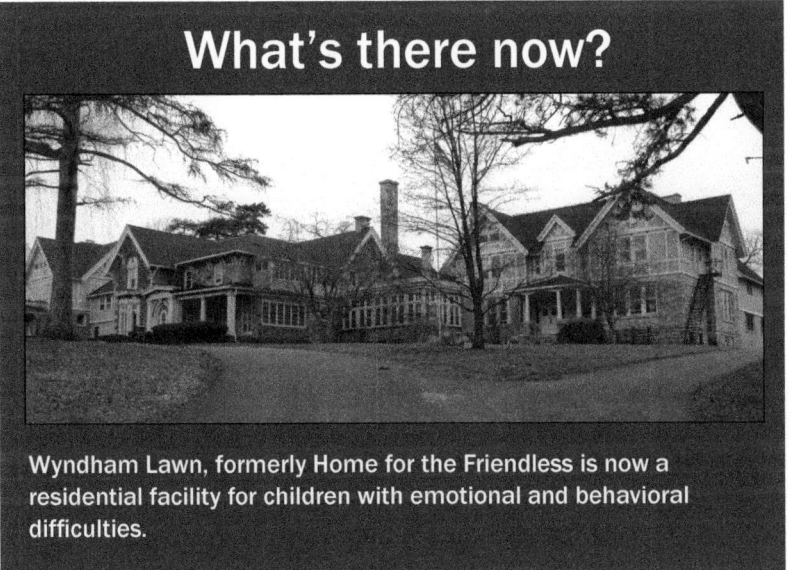

What's there now?

Wyndham Lawn, formerly Home for the Friendless is now a residential facility for children with emotional and behavioral difficulties.

The Flagler Emergency Hospital
291 West Avenue
Lockport, NY
1888-1908

This was the start of the Lockport City Hospital, in a house donated by Thomas T. Flagler in 1888. In 1889, the management of the hospital was turned over to the Lockport Board of Health. The hospital operated until 1908 until the Lockport City Hospital at 521 East Ave, Lockport NY, opened. The property at 291 West Avenue was then returned to Thomas T. Flagler's estate.

Initially the organizational structure and management came under the scrutiny of the Charity Organization Society[3] and a meeting was held with the representative of The Kings Daughters[4], The Charity Organization Society, and The Board of Health, where the new structure and by-laws for the corporation were approved.

Flagler Emergency Hospital – 291 West Avenue, Lockport, New York.

Flagler Hospital

RULES OF THE BOARD OF HEALTH FOR THE GOVERNMENT THEROF.

[Adopted May 7, 1889, and ratified by the Common Council May 13, 1889.]

WHEREAS, The gift of the Flagler Hospital was the
A charity beginning of a Christian charity that is
destined, if properly managed, to be a lasting benefit
and credit to the city; therefore, be it

Resolved, That in the opinion of this board of health the Flagler Hospital was not provided for such cases as are the proper wards of the county house, or to encourage genteel pauperism; but especially to provide a suitable retreat for such as are strangers in the city and are accidentally injured by any cause, or suddenly seized with acute diseases; all travelers or servants in hotels, or in private families, who are suffering from contagious or infectious diseases and have neither city homes nor welcome shelter, and are too sick to be removed to their own or friendly homes, excepting such as are suffering from small-pox. This hospital shall be opened to the foregoing classes on making proper application to the board of health.

Lockport, New York Common Council Resolution, 1889

Documents of the Senate of the State of New York, Volume 7.
By New York (State), Legislature, Senate.

State Board of Charities

HOSPITALS.
FLAGLER EMERGENCY HOSPITAL, 291 West Avenue, Lockport, N.Y.

Established September, 1888.

Objects. – Emergency cases.
Governing body. – Board of Health.
President. – Calvin G. Sutliff, Lockport, N. Y.
Secretary. – T. U. Van Valkenburgh, Lockport, N. Y.
Treasurer. – J. C. Harrington, Lockport, N. Y.
Matron. – Mrs. Ella M. Farley.
Value of Property, $2,500.

    Number of patients cared for during the year, 13 (of this number 9 were paying patients and 4 beneficiaries); none remaining October 1, 1898.
    Receipts for the year ending September 30, 1898, including balance on hand ($377.35), $577.35; expenditures, $339.48; balance on hand October 1, 1898, $237.87.
    Terms and qualifications for admittance. – In accordance with rules of Board of Health.
    Application to be made to Committee on Hospital.

Documents of the Senate of the State of New York, Volume 7.
By New York (State), Legislature, Senate.

1870s-1906   109

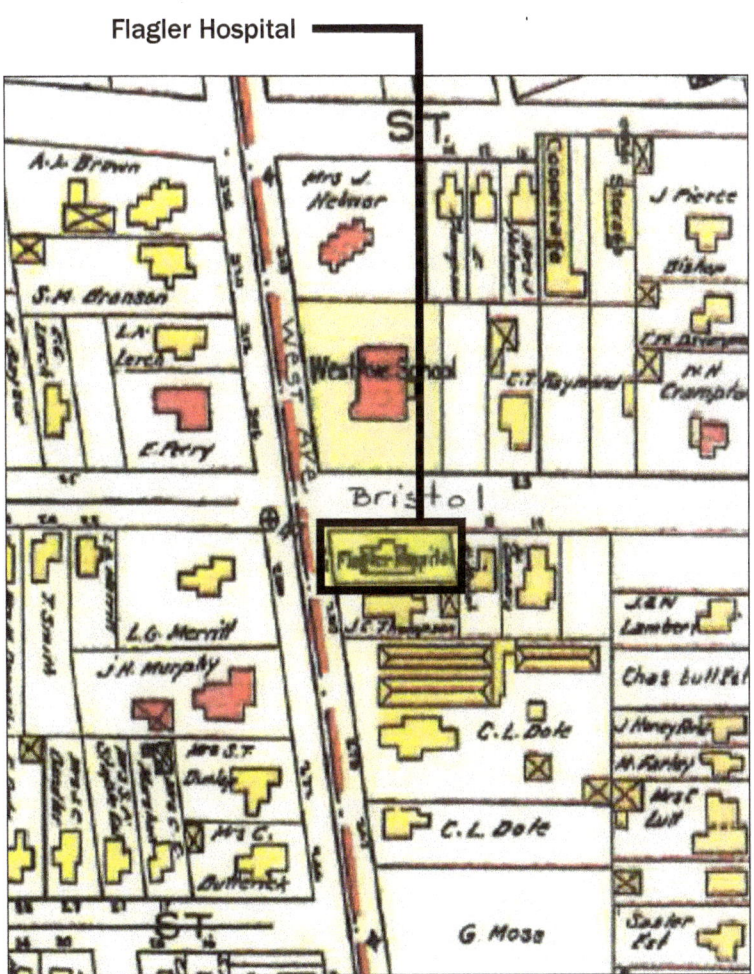

Flagler Hospital, Lockport, 1908.

Fort Niagara Hospital
Youngstown, New York
1890–1965

The fort's hospital and the nearby communities of Youngstown, Lewiston, and Porter were closely connected. Although not well documented, there is a locally known history of care for area residents living near the Fort Niagara Hospitals.

In 1914 an article from the *Syracuse Journal* covered a car accident that eventually took the life of eighteen-year-old Marjorie Webster. All six of the injured passengers were taken to Fort Niagara Hospital for treatment. An announcement in the February 23, 1931, *Niagara Falls Gazette* noted, "William DeVinney, who has been confined to the Fort Niagara Hospital for several days, is recovering."

An announcement on March 16, 1939, notes that the fort hospital provided care for Russell Diez, 27, manager of the Silverberg Farm on Lake Road. "Diez was first removed to the Fort Niagara Hospital where his injuries were diagnosed." Dr. Lewis W. Falkner of Youngstown was the attending physician.

Fort Niagara Hospital, 1895. Dr. William J. Falkner of Lewiston and Dr. Raymond, post doctor, are in the buggy.

Fort Niagara had many on-site hospitals during its 285 year history. During the period researched, 1914–1939, a review of the local *Niagara Falls Gazette* showed that local citizens received care for births, tractor/farm accidents, automobile injuries, and pneumonia at the fort's hospital.

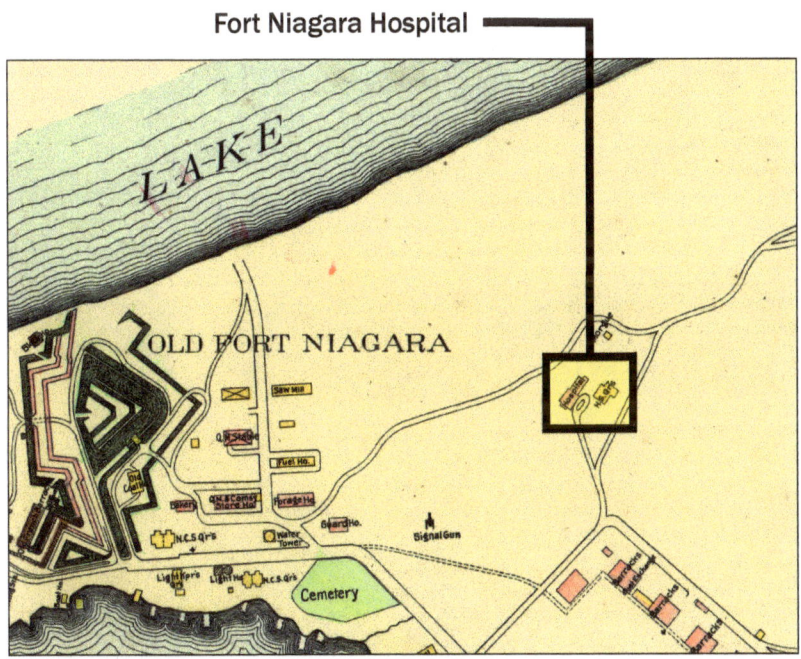

Fort Niagara military reservation, 1908.

Hospital Timeline

1890: Brick hospital built.

1914–1924: Wood mess hall and kitchen added to brick hospital.

1917–1921: Fire destroyed part of the hospital, but it was rebuilt.

1917–1931: Hospital isolation ward (quarantine wing) built.

What's there now?

Park and picnic grounds are located where the old fort hospital once stood.

The Charity Organization Society
1891

Founded February 6th, 1891, with an office in room 12 of the old Lockport YMCA at 106 Main Street at the corner of Locust, the Charity Organization Society of the City of Lockport, New York was created, according to their publications, "to secure the harmonious co-operation of the different charities of the city". Founding members were John E. Pound, Willis H. Howes, Wallace I. Keep, Mrs. F.N. Trevor, Miss Catharine Fitch, Miss Alice M. Pomroy.

The first Charity Organization Society in the United States was established in Buffalo, New York in 1877. The Lockport society (1891) was the first Charity Organization Society in Niagara County with the Niagara Falls society incorporating in 1895. These groups were formed in many cities from 1880's-into the 1920's. Most progressed and became service organization or were folded into early versions of the Community Chest and United Way.

Charity Organization Societies, were a "scientific" effort to eliminate poverty, make sure charity money was spent wisely and enhance family life. In the 1892 annual meeting minutes of the group, the Lockport society investigator, Mrs. Lena Burge's report exposed "several of the frauds the charitable public have been subjected…". The Charity Organization Societies were worried about "pauperizing" those receiving assistance and it was felt that charity could cause those receiving care and their families to become dependent on the aid and not become productive members of society. The goal was for the recipients to become self-supporting.

The Provident Wood Yard Mission and Day Care
1893-1896

The Provident Wood Yard Mission was a charity organization that operated at 114 Church Street, Lockport, New York. A number of cities started a Provident Wood Yard, and they could be found in Buffalo, Boston, and Chicago. The Provident Wood Yard had a unique plan to help the unfortunate, the needy were enlisted to cut and chop wood which was then sold as stove wood or kindling. According to Miss E. Peterson, Secretary of the organization, "Each applicant, not disabled, is required to saw and split a certain amount of wood for his meal or lodging". The wood yard provided the mission with operating funds, productive work for those needing help, and helped deflect the concern that the poor were not worthy of assistance. The mission also included a day care for mothers who had to work. Self-described as a "Food and Shelter Mission" according to the December 1893 monthly report, 134 meals, lodging for 51, and 61 children were cared for in the nursery. The organization operated at this address from 1893-1896. The property was ¾ of an acre that

Location of Provident Wood Yard Mission, 114 Church Street., Lockport New York.

was once owned by Lockport businessman, G.W. Hildreth. It included an iron foundry, shop buildings and a large house.

Provident Wood Yard Mission.

GIVE US A HELPING HAND.

Right at your own door is a mission to the poor, the hungry and the homeless; those who would be compelled to beg from door to door, but for this home of mercy.

This Food and Shelter Mission is known as the **Provident Wood Yard**, and is open every day, at **No. 114 Church St.**, where you are requested to send all who come to your door for help.

Give us your **subscription** to this practical charity, which knows neither nationality nor creed, and BUY OUR WOOD.

BOARD OF MANAGERS.

MRS. CHAS. KEEP, MRS. H. S. BEVERLY, MISS LOUNSBURY,
" HERRICK, " WILLIS HOWES, MRS. J. E. POUND,
" A. H. IVINS, MISS WHITMORE, " H. J. STEPHENSON
" D. VAN SHULER, MRS. W. W. WELLS, " JAMES LIDDLE,
" JAMES COMPTON, " ALBERT HELMER, " JAMES CARTER,
" J. CARL JACKSON, " REUBEN CARROL, " F. K. SWEET,
" F. J. SAWYER, MISS E. HELMER, —MISS E. PETERSON.
MRS. A. R. FERGUSON.

Independent Order of Odd Fellows Homes
Lockport, New York
1894

The Independent Order of Odd Fellows is a benevolent fraternity that helps the poor and cares for the needy.

The original Odd Fellows home and farm was for aged Odd Fellow members, their wives, widows, and orphans. The main house opened in 1894 and was known as Wood Lawn.

Wood Lawn was a spacious, eighty-acre fruit farm and house, complete with steam heat and electric lights. Stock and machinery were purchased for the farm, providing much of the food needed by the home. Proceeds from the farm were the primary source of revenue. All residents had a job, no matter how small, contributing to the functioning of the home.

In 1907 a small nearby farm was purchased from a Mr. Luremen for use as an orphanage. This fifty-two-acre property included a home and barnyard and was dedicated on August 1, 1907.

Wood Lawn in 1894. The original Odd Fellows home and farm for aged Odd Fellow members, their wives, widows, and orphans was located on Old Niagara Road and Lake Avenue, Lockport.

1870s-1906   127

Main kitchen, Odd Fellows Home, Lockport.

Interior of the original home.

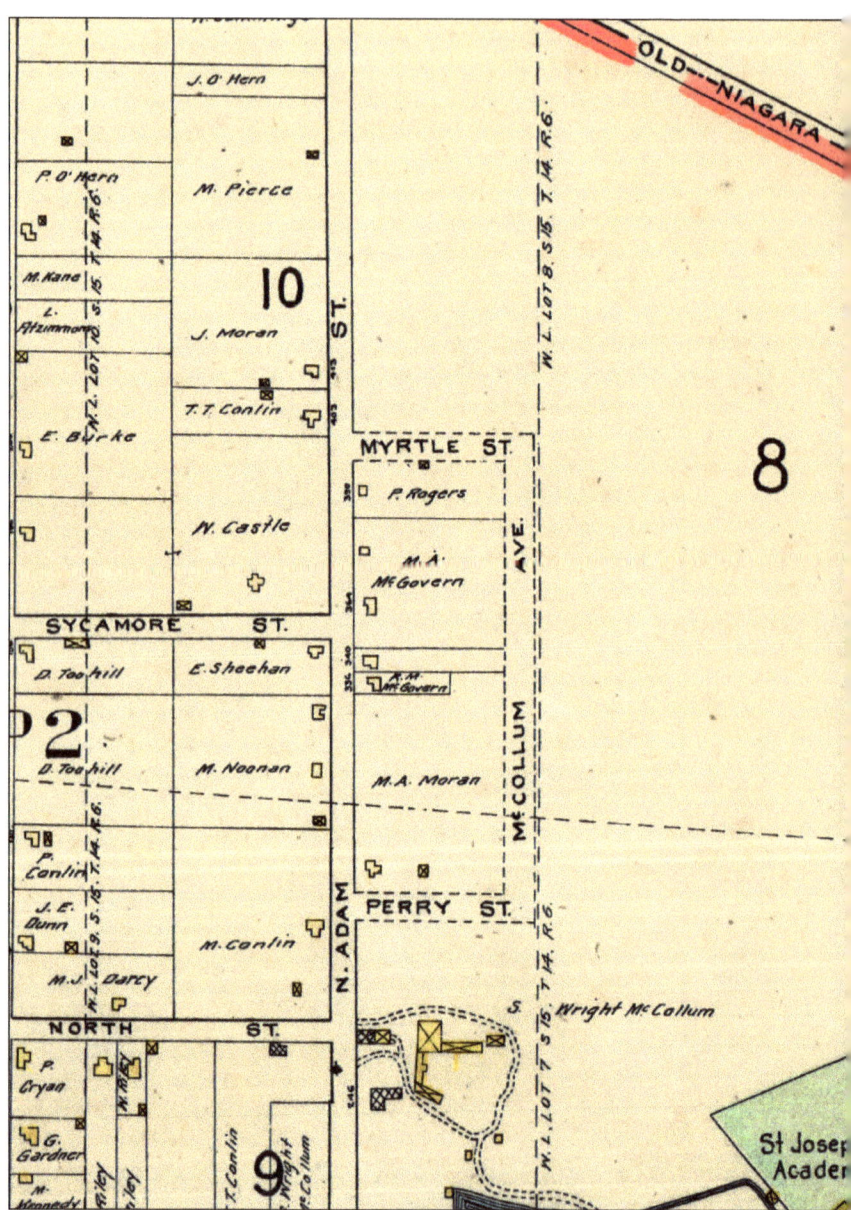

Independent Order of Odd Fellows Home and Independent Order of Odd Fellows Home Orphanage, Lockport, 1908.

1870s-1906   129

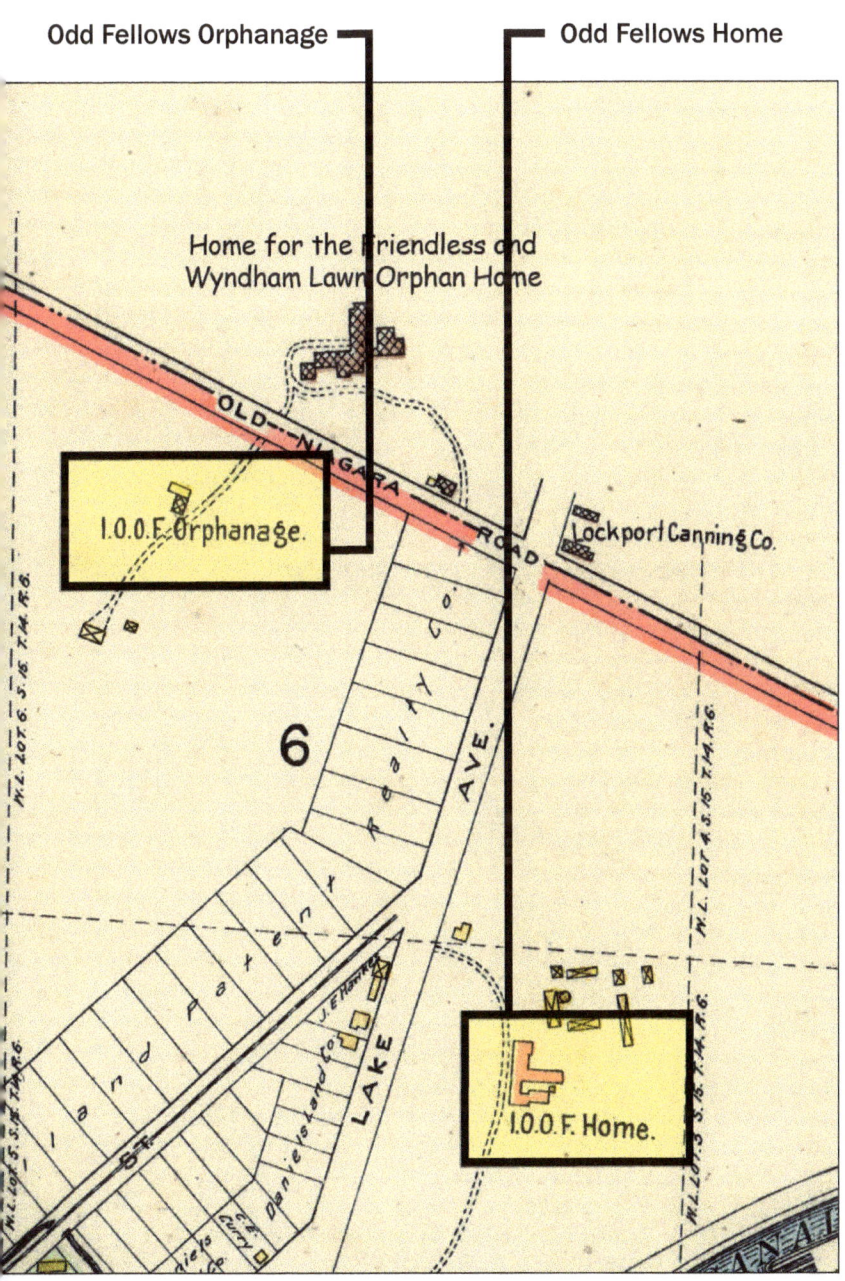

Odd Fellows Orphan Home, Old Niagara Road and Lake Avenue, Lockport.

HOMES FOR THE AGED.

ODD FELLOWS HOME ASSOCIATION OF THE STATE OF NEW YORK, Lockport, Niagara County, N. Y.

Incorporated May 5, 1893.

Objects.—To purchase a home for, and to support and maintain aged and indigent Odd Fellows and destitute widows and orphans of deceased members. (As yet, only the Adult Department is organized).

Governing body.—Managers.
President.—Hon. Charles Hickey, Lockport, N. Y.
Secretary.—J. M. Deyo, 8 Maple Place, Rochester, N. Y.
Treasurer.—F. F. Lansill, 2462 Main street, Buffalo, N. Y.
Superintendent.—George W. Haynes.
Value of property, $29,769.81.
Number of aged cared for during the year, 21; remaining October 1, 1898, 14.

Receipts for the year ending September 30, 1898, including balance on hand ($1,391.65), $8,818.88; expenditures, $8,304.07; balance on hand October 1, 1898, $514.81.

Qualifications for admittance.—A member of the order, 60 years of age, totally unable to support himself or herself, from lack of means, or disability is received.

Application to be made to the Association through his or her lodge.

Excerpt taken from the *Annual Report of the State Board of Charities of the State of New York*, 1898.

Children of the Odd Fellows Orphan Home, Old Niagara Road and Lake Avenue, Lockport.

Fraternal Orders and Insurance
The Odd Fellows were early pioneers in establishing life, health, and injury insurance that its lodges provided to members. Members and their families were never to become a public charge. With the creation of modern government programs and products from insurance companies, Odd Fellows eventually phased out their programs.

Odd Fellows Home Association of New York Located at Lockport

The Odd Fellows Home at Lockport is under an Association independent of the Grand Lodge of New York. It was organized in 1893, incorporated May 5, 1893, and re incorporated August 4, 1903.

There are two Homes under the Association—one for aged Odd Fellows, their wives and widows. This is located on a fine fruit farm of eighty acres. On a nearby fruit farm of fifty acres, is the Orphans Home. Fifty eight acres of this property are within the city limits and can be reached by electric street cars.

The Main Home is complete in all its appointments heated with steam and lighted with electricity. Recently new additions were made to the Adult Home, consisting of dining room, well equipped kitchen and serving room with new fittings. The new laundry, ice plant and refrigerating system, gas stoves and ovens, have helped in providing clean, wholesome living for our large family in a most satisfactory and economical manner.

The management is under a Board of Trustees, with a Superintendent for the farms, and a Matron for each of the two Homes. Everything is moving along in a modern and satisfactory manner.

Excerpt taken from *Album of Odd Fellows Homes*, 1927.

1870s-1906 133

Odd Fellows Orphan Home, 1910

Page No. 127

Department of Commerce and Labor-Bureau of the Census
THIRTEENTH CENSUS OF THE UNITED STATES: 1910 - POPULATION
NY STATE - NIAGARA COUNTY

Name of Incorporated Place: City of Lockport NY

The name of every person	Age	Sex	Color White, Black or Mulatto	Relationship of this person to head of family	Profession, Occupation or Trade of each person	Place of Birth	
1	2	3	4	5	6	7	
Murphy, Anna M				Wife	Matron		8
Murphy, James					Husband		9
Cook, Harriett					Domestic Orphanage		10
Smith, Irene F.	14	F	W			New York	11
Smith, Pearl	10	F	W			New York	12
Smith, George M	9	M	W			New York	13
Smith, William M	7	M	W			New York	14
Sturdevant, Kenneth M	13	M	W			New York	15
Sturdevant, Clara F	9	F	W			New York	16
Sturdevant, Jesse M	5	M	W			New York	17
							18
							19
							20
							21

Transcribed from the *1910 U.S. Census of Lockport, Niagara County* (Edition 78, page 127, Sheet 11A, 1st District, 2nd Ward).

What's there now?

The original Odd Fellows Home served both adults and children. It is now called the Odd Fellow and Rebekah Rehabilitation and Health Care Center, located at 104 Old Niagara Road in Lockport.

The former orphan home before renovations. It is located on the southwest corner of Lake Avenue (Route 78) and old Niagara Road, Lockport.

Interior of the former orphan home, 2016. The wood floors are original to the house.

Interior of the former orphan home, 2016. The stone wall is original to the house.

Charity Organization Society (Family and Children's Service of Niagara, Inc.) Niagara Falls, New York 1895–2011

The Charity Organization Society is an older human service agency that has survived and adapted as the needs of the local community changed. Through World Wars I and II, the worldwide flu epidemic of 1918, downturns in the economy like the Great Depression of 1929, and the ups and downs of business cycles in a manufacturing town, the society provided assistance to people in need. Located on the border with Canada, the agency also provided services to a large number of immigrants (1895–1959) who relocated to Niagara Falls for employment. One of the earlier national programs, Traveler's Service Society, was first established to assist young women who were moving to cities for employment. It later evolved to help individuals and families in transition and travelers with border-crossing issues.

Former headquarters of Charity Organization Society, 1912–2010, which is now known as Family and Children's Service of Niagara Inc. The building is located at 826 Chilton Avenue, Niagara Falls.

> **ITS OBJECTS AND MEMBERSHIPS DEFINED**
> The meeting of the Charity Organization Tuesday morning was well attended and much enthusiasm was shown by those present. The committee appointed to draw up a constitution made their report and the constitution was adopted. The Association's work is to be completely severed from all religious beliefs, politics, and nationality. It's objects are:
> - To be a center of intercommunication between the various charitable agencies in the city
> - To prevent children from growing up as paupers
> - To encourage thrift through friendly intercourse
> - To help the poor to help themselves, prevent begging
> - To provide that the case of applications for relief be thoroughly investigated, and the result of such investigations given the public poor officer, church, and charitable societies, and to charitable persons
> - To obtain employment, if possible, and so far as necessary give suitable assistance to every deserving applicant.[5]

From the *Niagara Falls Journal*, December 13, 1895.

The First Charity Organization Societies

The first in the United States was established in Buffalo, New York, in 1877. Originally founded in Europe, the Buffalo society was developed by the Reverend S. H. Gurteer who modeled it after a similar organization in London.

Charity Organization Societies were formed in many cities from the 1880s into the 1920s. Many progressed and became service organizations or were folded into early versions of the Community Chest and United Way.[6]

Charity Organization Societies, a "scientific" effort to eliminate poverty and enhance family life, are credited with the professionalism of social work. An early clearinghouse for care in communities, the organization's primary goal was coordinating

> The organization went through many name changes:
> - The Charity Organization Society of Niagara Falls, 1895
> - Social Service League, 1915
> - Family Welfare Society, 1938
> - Family and Children's Society, 1940s
> - Family and Children's Services, 1970s
> - Family and Children's Service of Niagara, Inc.[7]

charity in a geographic area. The New York City Charity Organization Society and the Russell Sage Foundation's Charity Organization Department assisted many of the societies by disseminating information with publications and conferences.[8]

Early Years of the Niagara Falls Charity Organization Society

The first meeting of the Niagara Falls Charity Organization Society was held at the Gluck Building in 1895. Initial funding came from Gorge Road, Niagara Falls, and Suspension Bridge railroad companies. O. W. Cutler, editor of *The Daily Cataract*, called the first meeting of sixteen volunteer women and assisted in organizing the Society.[10] Staff members were unpaid until 1925.

> The ladies of this city interested in charitable work have organized an association and elected these officers: President -- Mrs. E S Nichols; Vice Presidents -- Mrs. H E Woodford, Mrs. Thomas Gaskin, and Mrs. C B Gaskil; Secretary -- Mrs. Arthur McClanathan; Treasurer -- Mrs. Max Amberg.
>
> The action of the earnest women in organizing for such a noble cause is deserving of the highest commendation, and of the greatest encouragement in their work.[9]

From the *Niagara Falls Journal*, December 6, 1895.

The Value of a Quarry

Organizations that helped the poor and needy were faced with having to justify the use of charity and public money. The charity organization societies were specifically created to frugally coordinate aid in a given geographical area with the goal of eventually eliminating poverty.

Often social service agencies either leased quarries or had stone delivered to stone-yards located on-site. Recipients of care were obliged to break stone for use in building projects or roads. Almost everyone could work in a stone-yard. Social service agencies considered the work an ideal way to deflect public views that some recipients were not worthy of help.

> There was a similar society in nearby Buffalo, the Buffalo Charity Organization society, which was the first organized charity organization in the United States. They maintained a stoneyard where unemployed were given a chance to earn money by crushing stone. The Niagara Falls women considered this a good idea but when the Committee on Employment and Protection tried to get the City Council to appropriate a piece of property for a stone yard, the council disagreed. The women were not discouraged by the refusal but spent many hours trying to get action on their proposal.

The 1895 annual report of the Charity Organization Society of Niagara Falls discussed the need for a stoneyard.

No. 45.–Italian, aged thirty in 1910; children eight, seven, three years and one born after application. Mr. I was a tailor's helper earning $9 to $12 a week, his work often being irregular. The family had lived in two rooms for which they paid $5 a month rent. Mr. I died in 1910 from appendicitis, leaving no insurance, but Mrs. I had some savings on which she lived for a few weeks. A subscription of $89 raised by friends paid for the funeral. Three weeks after his death Mrs. I applied to the C. O. S. She was unable to work because of her approaching confinement, and the city agreed to give $3 a week and coal in winter, and a private agency $2 a week. This regular allowance is to continue until the baby is old enough to permit Mrs. I to work. The three older children are all small and backward, but the new baby seems healthy. An Italian friendly visitor is in close touch with the family, and is teaching Mrs. I how to sew.

An excerpt from *A Study of 985 Widows Known to Certain Charity Organization Societies in 1910*. This is an early example of the "scientific" study of poverty and family issues, authored by Mary E. Richmond and Fred S. Hall, and published by the Charity Organization Department, Russell Sage Foundation, New York.

1870s-1906   143

The Junior League Volunteer Motor Corps, of which Mrs. Thomas Coyle is chairman, delivering boxes of remade clothing to the Family Welfare Society for distribution to the worthy poor of the city.

Helping out during the Depression in 1931. The Family Welfare Society was an early name for Family and Children's Service of Niagara, Inc.

144　Chapter 2

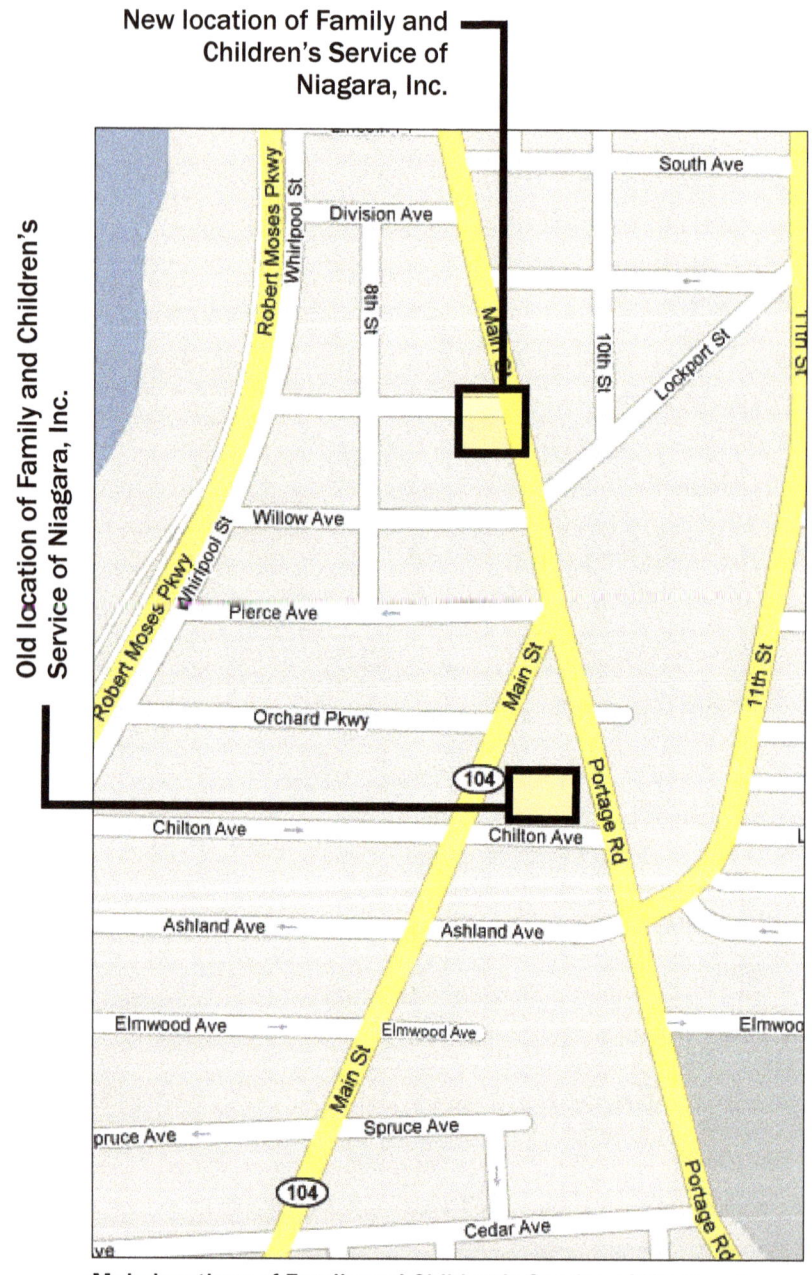

Main locations of Family and Children's Service of Niagara, Inc., Niagara Falls.

Locations of the main offices of the organization in Niagara Falls[10]
- 1895: Arcade Building, Room 4, Falls Street
- 1907: 2118 Main Street
- 1938: 826 Chilton Avenue
- 2011: 1522 Main Street

What's there now?

Family and Children's Service of Niagara, Inc. headquarters building. Now with offices in Buffalo, Lockport, Lewiston, and North Tonawanda and services throughout Western New York, the agency continues to serve and support families and children with the following programs: domestic violence services, an employee assistance program, Healthy Families Niagara, mental health, and runaway youth services.

Villa St. Vincent
Youngstown, New York
1904–1954

Villa St. Vincent was the summer home for students of St. Vincent's Female Orphan Asylum and Technical School in Buffalo.

From 1904 this large summer complex overlooking the Niagara River was owned and operated by the Roman Catholic Order of the Sisters of Charity of the Sisters of St. Vincent de Paul. The structures on the property included ten buildings for daily living, recreation, and worship. Piers located at the water's edge allowed for recreational activities throughout the summer, including boating. The children helped with daily chores at the villa.

After 1951 Villa St. Vincent was managed by the Sisters of Charity Hospital of Buffalo for the benefit of girls from the Good Shepherd Home.

Villa St. Vincent was razed in 1957, although the chapel, still in good repair, was relocated. Now used as a parish hall, it stands on the grounds of St. John's Episcopal Church on Main and Chestnut Streets in Youngstown.

B. 451. Villa St. Vincent, Youngstown, N. Y.

Villa St. Vincent, Main and Jackson Streets, Youngstown.

> It was clean and well run and there was a schedule of work and things to do. The nuns took care of us, but they were formal, and it's not that they didn't care, but I think they were trained to be standoffish. However, you could tell that some had their favorites even though all of us girls were fairly treated."

Mary J. Bohmhauer, a former orphan who spent summers at Villa St. Vincent, in a 2010 interview.

NIAGARA COUNTY — PRIVATE CHARITY.

FRESH AIR CHARITIES.

VILLA ST. VINCENT,

Youngstown, N. Y.

Established 1906.

Summer home of ST. VINCENT'S FEMALE ORPHAN ASYLUM, 1138 Ellicott street, Buffalo, N. Y.

The children are taken to the country at the close of the school year and remain until the end of the first week in August. Later on the girls of the technical department of the Asylum are given a rest at the Villa.

Governing body.— Board of Managers of parent institution.
Superintendent.— Sister Mary Gabriel.
Finances and statistics included with parent institution.
One hundred and twenty-eight girls were given six weeks' vacation in this country home.
Census on day of inspection, 134, all public charges.
For general information concerning parent institution, see *Homes for Children*, Erie County.

Excerpt taken from the *Annual Report of the State Board of Charities for the Year 1916*.

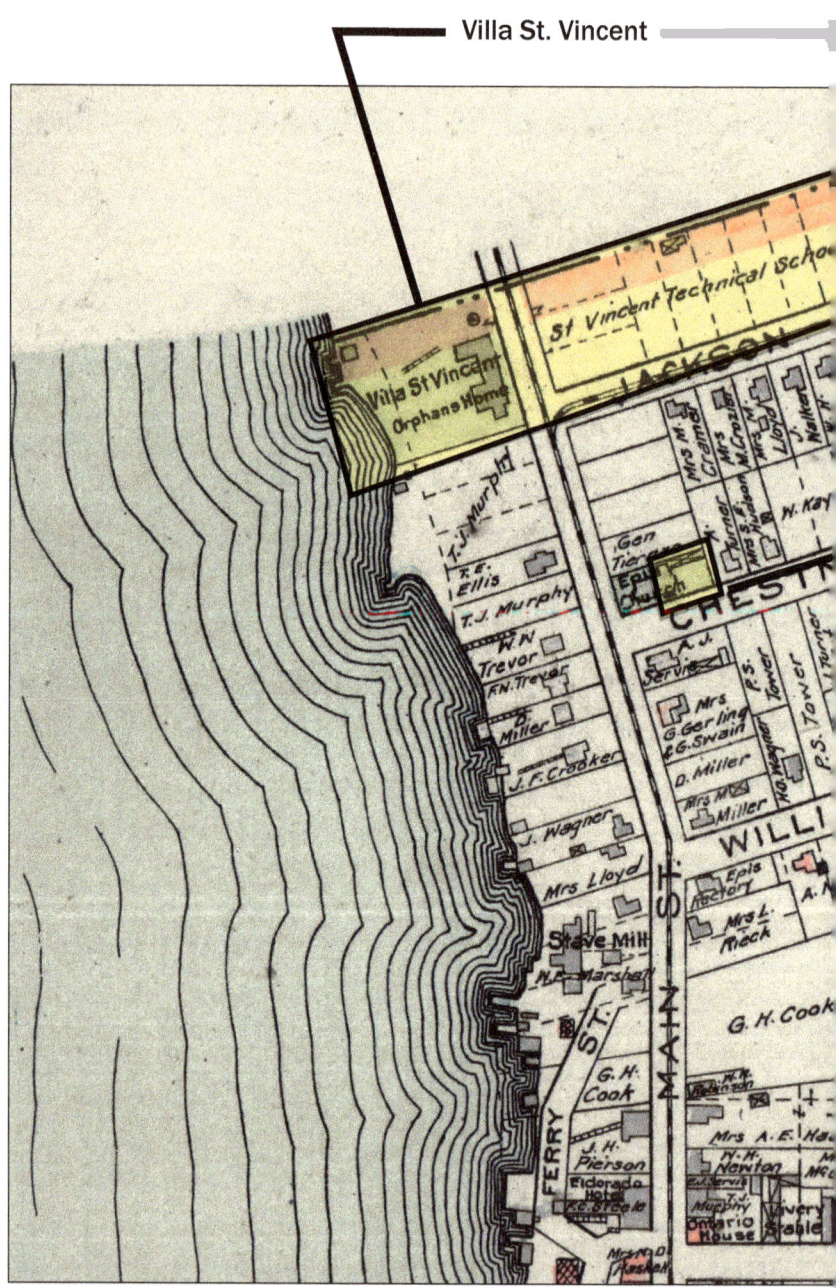

Location of Villa St. Vincent, Youngstown, 1908.

Villa St. Vincent Chapel

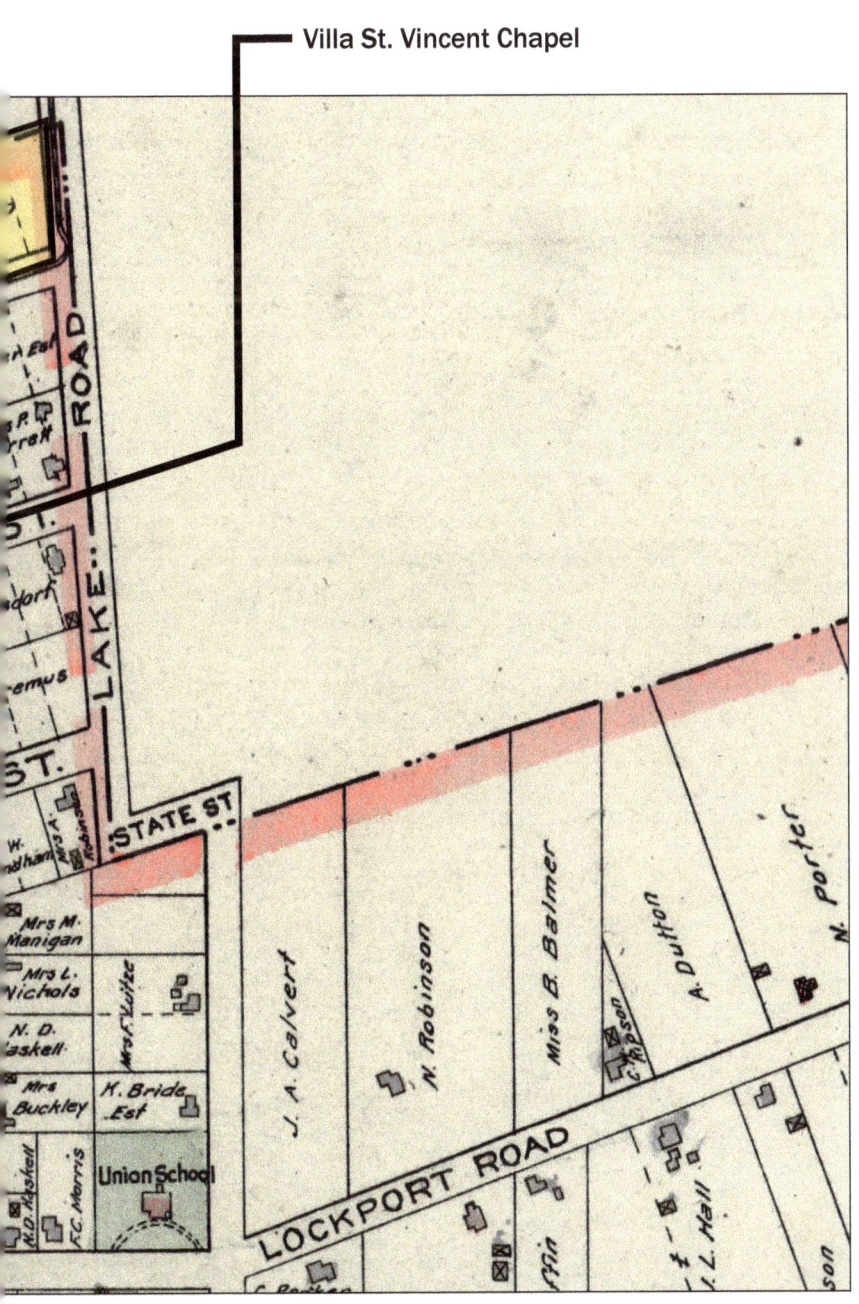

Villa St. Vincent on the Niagara River. Twin steps led to two piers, one set of steps for the grade school, one for the high school.

An early photograph of Villa St. Vincent Chapel, Youngstown.

1870s-1906   153

Villa St. Vincent, Youngstown. A large statue of Mary faced the water.

Villa St. Vincent Chapel being moved to its new location.

> "Sally was one of the orphans from St. Vincent's Female Orphan Asylum in Buffalo, who came here to Youngstown for the summers from 1925 to 1938. Sally was born Nov. 1919, and was one of four children. Her mother died when she was four, and the siblings were looked after by their relatives for a period of time. Eventually it became apparent that her father could not work and keep the family together, so three of the children were put in the orphan asylum with their father visiting from time to time. Getting to the Villa from Buffalo was quite an adventure. The girls sat in a 'paddy wagon' with seats on each side and a bench in the middle. When they came to Lewiston Hill, they all prayed that the brakes would work and they did not end up with a runaway wagon. The youngest was aged five and the oldest was eighteen years. Sally remembers 100 girls."

Conversation with Sally (Cecelia) LaPlante Aseltine at the Town of Porter Museum on November 5, 2009. Town of Porter Historical Society, History Files.

What's there now?

River view of former Villa St. Vincent location.

Niagara Falls Quarantine Hospital (Municipal Hospital)
Niagara Falls, New York
1906–1950

The Niagara Falls Quarantine Hospital was located on Porter Road, southwest of 29th Street (Marcia Street on older maps). It was established in 1906 to be used as a quarantine hospital when the pest house on Pine Avenue near Portage Road was closed due to community opposition.

The hospital started with four beds and had live-in caretakers. It operated under the health officer and city manager, who reported to the Niagara Falls City Council. The hospital employed graduate nurses supervised by the hospital superintendent.

> *The thirty-eight bed quarantine hospital treated a total of 156 cases of communicable diseases in 1919.*

In 1910, two new buildings were added. The thirty-eight bed quarantine hospital treated a total of 156 cases of communicable diseases in 1919. In 1922, it became the Niagara Falls Municipal Hospital.

Patients' quarters were located in the wings of the frame house next to the brick administration building. Porter Road and 29th Street, Niagara Falls, 1946.

The City of Niagara Falls hired hospital consultant Dr. Basil C. McLean to review the hospitals of the city. He found the Municipal Hospital too costly to operate per patient and no longer needed, as described in an account on the subject: "Immunization and improved public health procedures had reduced the incidence of contagious disease, and segregated pest houses were a folly and extravagance."[11]

The hospital closed on December 31, 1950. There are now several private homes on the corner property where the hospital once stood.

> In 1893, a structure on Pine Avenue near Portage Road, a "pest" house in the terminology of the day, accommodated such patients. In January 1897 Dr. Walter S. Scott, city health officer, reported that the "hospital" for contagious disease had been taken by the city for other purposes and "is now being moved away." By August, with no action taken, Dr. Scott again pointed up the problem and urged immediate steps to remedy the situation. In response, the Board of Health appointed a committee to select a site for the erection of a pest house.

A "looking back" article from the *Niagara Falls Gazette*, July 6, 1980.

Quarantine hospital
A hospital where sick people are quarantined. Quarantine is voluntary or compulsory isolation, typically to contain the spread of disease during an epidemic. Such hospitals were used to house those afflicted with communicable diseases such as cholera, smallpox, tuberculosis, and influenza.

160   Chapter 2

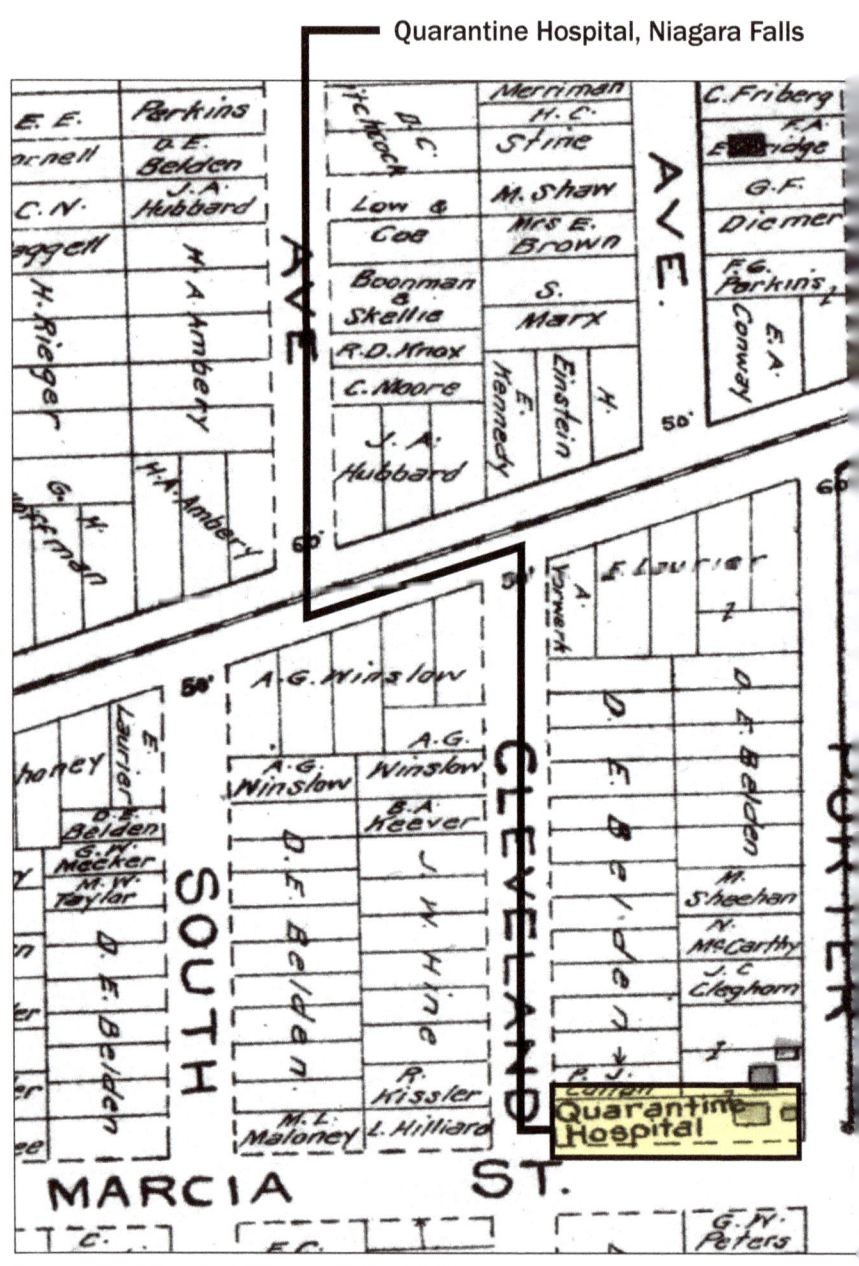

Quarantine Hospital, Niagara Falls, 1908.

1870s-1906 161

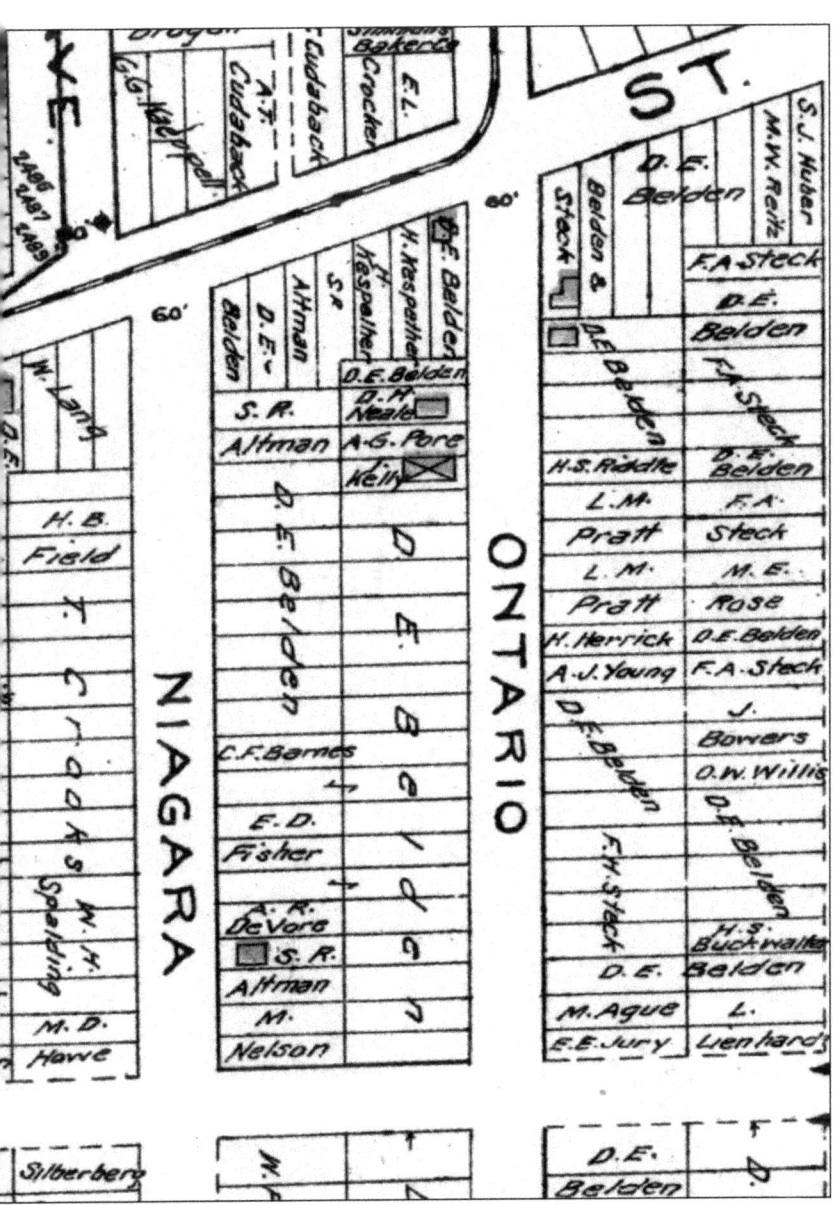

SMALLPOX BAD AT NIAGARA.

105 Cases There, and Disease Develops in Nine Other Places.

ALBANY, Feb. 14.—Lax methods of dealing with smallpox are responsible for 105 cases of it in Niagara Falls and the spread of the disease to nine more cities and villages within the last week, according to Dr. Lindsay Rudd Williams, Deputy Commissioner of Health. Thirty-nine houses in Niagara Falls are now under quarantine, he said, and twenty-two patients are being cared for in the quarantine hospital.

"Until Dr. Hermann M. Biggs, the Health Commissioner, took charge of the situation," said Dr. Williams, "the lax methods of control had resulted in the spread of the disease to twenty-seven cities and towns. Within the last week cases have been reported from Elmira, Dayton, Medina, Stockton, Porter, Villa Nova, Amherst, Wheatfield, and Portland, all towns in the Western part of the State. All these cases have been traced directly to Niagara Falls."

The New York Times, February 15, 1914.

DISPENSARY AND CLINIC SERVICE AT NIAGARA FALLS
Walter A. Scott, MD
Health Office, Niagara Falls, NY

While the recent United States census gives the city a population of but 50,760, the State Department of Health estimate is 53,899, and the directory census 60,000. It seems probable that this latter figure more nearly approaches the correct number of people within the city limits. It is estimated that at least 40 percent of the population of the city is foreign-born; one church alone has 10,000 communicants, practically all of whom are of this class...There are 376 factories located within the city limits. The average birth rate has always been one of the highest in the State. In 1919 it was 25.61. The mortality rate for children under one year per thousand births in 1919 was 110, the average rate for the State for during the same year being 89...

Of the three hospitals in the city, one, the Municipal Hospital, handles communicable diseases and is entirely supported by municipal appropriation. This hospital has a capacity of 38 beds and treats all communicable diseases except tuberculosis, and venereal diseases in male patients, it being impossible to take cases of the latter since there is no male orderly service. A total of 156 cases of communicable diseases were treated in the municipal hospital in 1919.

From the *Monthly Bulletin,* New York State Department of Health, Vol. 35-36 (page 172), 1919.

Sara Dale working in the kitchen at the quarantine hospital.

What's there now?

The old quarantine hospital, now removed, was located at the southwest corner of Porter Road and 29th Street extending down to Cleveland Avenue. There are houses on the property today.

CHAPTER 3
1908-1918

Stella Niagara
Stella Niagara, New York

Located just outside Youngstown, Stella Niagara, the administrative headquarters for the Sisters of St. Francis, was established in 1908. The name given to the property is from the Latin hymn, "Ave Maris Stella."

The first school opened in 1908. The campus, with a continuous focus on education, housed a grade school, high school, day and boarding school, and a cadet program for boys ages eight to fourteen. Today there is a day school for children ages three to fourteen.

Although the schools were generally for families that could afford to send their children to private schools, some children received financial assistance, and the tuition for orphans was often quietly paid for by the order.

> *The campus, with a continuous focus on education, housed a grade school, high school, day and boarding school, and a cadet program for boys ages eight to fourteen.*

Stella Niagara, 4421 Lower River Road, Stella Niagara.

Military cadet school classes, 1935–1936, Stella Niagara. From left to right are (first row) William Jackson, Charles Benzing, William Fitzpatrick, John Plunkett, Alfred Bobst, James Hines, Robert Zimmermann, Donald Murphy, Paul Holahan, and John Zimmermann; (second row) Francis McGreevy, Richard Leary, William Murphy, Joseph O'Donnell, Francis Kreuper, Joseph Arneth, James McGreevy, and Robert Roach; (third row) Frank Deck, Kenneth Hines, Thomas Guinan, Nathaniel Barone, Frank Offermann, Kenneth Smith, Emmit Glanz, and David Zimmermann; (fourth row) Gregory Deck, William Hallett, Teddy Hollinshead, Francis Meyers, Raymond Kersten, John Mumm, and Gerard Zimmermann; (fifth row) Major Curtis of Fort Niagara, Edward Guenther, William McGreevy, George Moran, Thomas Quinn, and Sergeant Rosenberg of Fort Niagara.

Due to the Sisters of St. Francis' philosophy, their acts of kindness were considered private, making it difficult to research their contributions. One member of the order noted in a scrapbook that "Records of goodwill have never been kept in our archival history. Even our service to vagrants—knights of the road—as we call them, is never spotlighted in any way."[1] Stella Niagara continues its quiet tradition of offering a meal or a night's lodging to hungry travelers, a home for refugees awaiting papers for a border crossing, and temporary employment for immigrants and indigents.

What's there now?

Stella Niagara. The campus is still active with a day school (ages three to fourteen), residential health facility, and a center for private group retreats.

Buffalo State Hospital
Wilson Farm Colony
1908

In 1908, the Buffalo Psychiatric Hospital opened the Lakeside Colony on property leased from the Dwight family in Wilson, New York. The Colony operated for a little over four years and consisted of a small farm with a stone house and farm buildings in the village of Wilson, New York. With access to Lake Ontario, the Wilson farm provided the patients from Buffalo State Hospital recreation in the form of swimming, fishing, gardening, farming and outings to the nearby shops in the village.

It was reported in the Annual Report to the State Commission in Lunacy, 1909-1910, that 44 patients were housed at the Colony. Also in that year, the farm produced crops valued at $733.98, much of which was sent to the main Buffalo Hospital for use.[2]

In 1909 the farm was open the whole year to ease overcrowding at the Buffalo Hospital and 77 men and 74 women were housed at the Colony.

The hospital sent some of its convalescent patients to the Wilson farm for two weeks at a time during summer months, where they would stay in the old stone house. It was believed

Farm Colony 1909, 81 Lake Street, Wilson, New York. Note the large fishing poles – The present owners stated that they found long fishing poles in the basement rafters when they remodeled the house in the 1980s.[3,4]

that escaping from Buffalo to the fresh country air afforded great benefit, "giving a place where the eye is not stopped in its outward look by the grim walls of factories, or in its upward search by the smoke of a great city."[5] The convalescent patients were able to "do as they like and the fresh air and liberty do them more good than anything else could…the percentage of cures among these patients has been most gratifying and the evident of all very marked."[6] It was considered a successful experiment. In another nearby house rooms were rented to house the men who stayed at the farm to work in the garden. A husband and wife were employed as caretakers.

Mentioned in the 40th Annual Report of the Buffalo State

Wilson Farm Colony, 81 Lake Ave., Wilson, New York.

Early picture of Farm Colony from state report.[7]

81 Lake Ave., Wilson, New York. Interior Wilson Farm Colony.

1908-1918   179

81 Lake Ave., Wilson, New York. Interior Wilson Farm Colony.

Pantry. 81 Lake Ave., Wilson, New York. Interior Wilson Farm Colony.

Fishing Pier and Bathing Beach Cottage for Patients. Wilson, New York, from early state reports.

Lake Ontario, Wilson, New York. Fishing Pier and Bathing Beach. This pier is found at the end of Rt. 425 (Lake Avenue).

Hospital was the high number of patients who found permanent employment in the nearby fruit farms. Also in this report, it was suggested that the farm not be purchased because the area was growing and it no longer would be a quiet retreat.[8]

The State Hospital tried for years to get permission from New York State to purchase the property for $6500 but it was never approved.[9] In April 1913, the farm was transferred to the private owner and the Buffalo State Hospital Annex in Wilson, New York closed.[10,11] More historical information about the Buffalo State Hospital Wilson Farm Colony can be found in the Richardson Olmstead Complex Cultural Landscape Report.[12]

The present owners, Chris Seiss and Jessica Hearst gave me a tour. There is a hidden stone room in the basement, blocked by an old bookcase with a sturdy door that is locked.

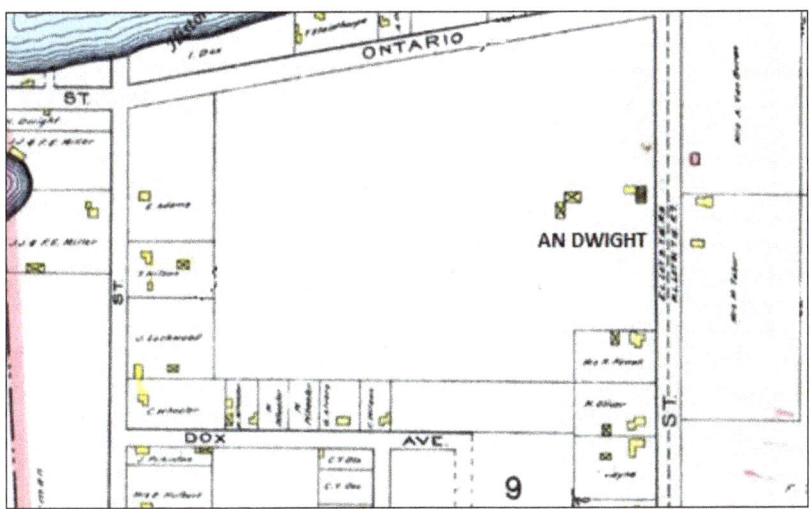

1908 map showing the A.N. Dwight farm, the location of Buffalo State Hospital Wilson Farm Colony.

Niagara County Infirmary
The "New" County Poorhouse
Lockport, New York
1915–1979

In 1912 the county decided to build a new poorhouse because the almshouse on Niagara Street Extension was deteriorating. It continued to experience water problems and flooding. Several large farms were purchased, including the Brown and Butler-Dempsey properties in east Lockport on Rogers Lane. The farm had a total of 174 acres. The Niagara County Infirmary was dedicated on January 7, 1915, to house the poor and indigent of Niagara County. With a capacity of 200 patients, the infirmary included an administration building, a service building, two men's buildings, one women's building, a hospital, several barns, and a hen house. Patients were transferred from the old poorhouse to the new infirmary on February 27, 1915.

Rogers Lane was also known as Lover's Lane. In 1918 the official name of the road was changed to Davison Road in honor of John Lester Davison, a local ornithologist and author of a book about birds.

Niagara County Infirmary, Davison Road, Lockport.

1908-1918 185

Fire at the County Home, 1955. Lockport *Union-Sun and Journal*.

Niagara County Infirmary Timeline 1908–2010

1908: A state charities report noted that the old almshouse should be replaced.

1912: A farm of 174 acres was purchased on Rogers Lane, now known as Davison Road, Lockport.

1915: The new facility was opened in January. The cost was $160,000, total capacity 200, hospital capacity 36.

Superintendent Jacob Shimer asked for "the employment of a cook, the enlargement of the kitchen, provision of a ward for those suffering with delirium tremens, and the building of a pest house for care of cases menacing the health of other inmates, and the employment of a herdsman," as he improved the infirmary.

In a 1929 Lockport *Union-Sun and Journal* article, Charles W. Walker, county superintendent of the poor, discussed the new terminology being adopted and said that the new laws would no longer use the term "poor." "Public welfare" would be the new term used when discussing issues related to the poor.

The Niagara County Infirmary expanded for the next thirty years. The Switzer Building, a new 120-bed infirmary, was added at a cost of $600,000 in 1950.

An article by Bill Nelson of the *Niagara Falls Gazette* in 1962 describes the typical residents of the infirmary as "county welfare cases too old to care for themselves or a few younger individuals who have exhausted their funds at other hospitals and still can hope for a future…and yet, the Infirmary is far from the grim or depressing place you might expect it to be."

Infirmary
A place where the infirm or sick are lodged for care and treatment.

1919: The Niagara infirmary served 93 residents: 60 men, and 33 women. Jacob Shimer was county superintendent of the poor.

1929–1950: New hospital beds were added, more farm land purchased, and a new chapel and men's building added.

1950: Switzer Building completed with a 120-bed hospital at a cost of $600,000.

Although past news articles discuss the stigma of living in a county poorhouse, the new administrator, Mrs. Lawrence Gaskill, put a more positive spin on the infirmary. "We try to make this a pleasant place to be, a place we wouldn't mind being in ourselves if we had to. The greatest change in the past twenty years is the fact that then everyone was in bed. Today, almost everyone is up and dressed every day."

During these years, the infirmary was almost at capacity. The staff consisted of 87 full-time and many part-time employees, including two physicians, a physiotherapist, dentist, occupational

Niagara County Infirmary and Social Services Department, 1950s.

1955: A large fire at the infirmary burned five barns, totaling $125,000 in damage.

1962 Census:
- 116 patients
- 64 men
- 52 women

1970s: Mrs. Gaskill was the administrator; capacity was 200 and the hospital was often near capacity. Ages ranged from 44–100.

therapist, activities director, dietitians, nurses, maintenance, and housekeeping.

Senior citizens visited twice a week. Welcome Wagon members visited often, and students of DeSales Catholic High School put on skits and took residents to the school for plays and musicals.

Niagara County government agencies gradually moved administrative departments to the infirmary property. The Parks Department, Social Services, and Civil Defense departments were using the buildings, along with the County Department of Weights and Measures.

After serving the county for 64 years, inspections in the 1970's reported the Infirmary did not meet current standards. To eliminate duplication of resources, services were consolidated with Mount View Hospital.

In June 1979 an article in the *Niagara Gazette* chronicles the infirmary's coming demise: "Infirmary on Davison Road being phased out." The infirmary was "too out of date" said George J. Needle, infirmary administrator. "Basically the building does not come up [to] the federal standard of nursing homes today."

No longer a nursing home or health-related facility, the Switzer building was renovated for office use. In 1979 the remaining patients and equipment were transferred to Mount View Hospital. The Switzer building housed the Niagara County Social Services Department from 1981 until 2003. Recently sections of the property were sold to a developer, which is in a zoning dispute.

1979: Infirmary does not meet health safety standards. Patients and equipment transferred to Mount View Hospital, according to George J. Needle, infirmary administrator.

2007: County lists property for sale at 4901 Davison Road: 17 acres with buildings, including a former home and infirmary.

2010: Property is owned by Niagara County and used for storage.

In the summer of 2021, there was a fire in the vacant chapel building. Several of the service buildings in the back are in use by Niagara County.

Potter's Field At The Infirmary (1915-1960)

The infirmary log book details burials in Potter's Field, an on-site cemetery for people buried at the government's expense. Most had been residents of the Niagara County Infirmary.

The graves at one time were marked by wooden crosses handmade by employees. As the wood disintegrated, metal markers were tried unsuccessfully, and over time the graves became unmarked. Potter's Field was closed to burials after June 30, 1960. All that remains today is a manicured lawn. Two headstones have been placed in the graveyard, one inscribed, "Niagara County Infirmary Cemetery, 1915–1960," the other "In memory of the children." Partial records can be found at the Niagara County Historian's Office or the Niagara County Historical Society, both on Niagara street, Lockport, New York.

Stone memorial for those buried in Potter's Field, the poorhouse cemetery, located on Davison Road, Lockport.

"In Memory of the Children" headstone.

Original infirmary plaque, 1915. Now located at the Niagara County Historical Society.

Abandoned doorway of the Niagara County Infirmary. This building was last used by the Social Services Department.

The First Tuberculosis Hospital

Niagara County Tuberculosis Hospital, Lockport, New York

Also known as Niagara County Sanatorium and Mount View

1915–2007

In 1910 the Niagara County Health Association led the initiative for a county hospital where tuberculosis could be treated. In a study commissioned by the association and completed in 1911, the severity of the tuberculosis epidemic in Niagara County was reported by the Niagara County Board of Supervisors, which voted to build a tuberculosis hospital in Lockport. In 1915 $100,000 was appropriated for the facility.

As a result of the County Health Association's efforts, a temporary tuberculosis hospital was set up in the old almshouse hospital, which was still located on the poorhouse grounds on Niagara Street Extension. In 1917 the building was moved up the hill, south to the newly purchased Niagara County Sanatorium property at 5465 Upper Mountain Road in Lockport. The building move was carried out by George Daunce & Son from Wilson, New York. The hospital building, now known as Pavilion #3, was remodeled with the addition of fresh-air porches.

Niagara County Sanatorium, first hospital building, 1918. The old almshouse hospital moved to Upper Mountain Road.

Overcrowding prompted the building of an additional facility for children named the Shaw Building in honor of Board of Managers member William Shaw. The Shaw Building opened on November 15, 1931, complete with dormitory, clinical facilities, and a school. In 1939 the Guillemont Building, a new adult building named in honor of Dr. Frank Guillemont, was added to the grounds. The recommended treatment for tuberculosis until the 1940s was diet, fresh air, exercise, and rest. It could take months, even years to recover.

After 1943 when streptomycin was discovered as a cure for tuberculosis, sanatoriums began to close. As a result, the Niagara Sanatorium became a multi-care health facility.

The facility was renamed Mount View Hospital on December 30, 1957, when the Shaw Building was renovated for a rehabilitation program for people with disabilities. The Shaw rehabilitation program included physical therapy, occupational therapy, rehabilitation nursing, vocational training, and speech and hearing therapy.

The top floor of the Guillemont Building was converted to a mental health ward in 1965. In 1972 Niagara County's Department of Social Services opened four foster homes for children ages thirteen to sixteen. The homes, former physicians' residences once part of the old Niagara County TB Sanitorium,

Sanitorium, Sanatorium or Sanitarium, Sanatarium
Health Resort or Hospital?
In general, if spelled with "or" (sanitorium), the facility most likely treated tuberculosis. Sanitarium is an older word for health resort, which provided fresh air, mineral waters, baths, and healthy food. Adding to the confusion, early tuberculosis hospitals often used health resort treatment methods, like fresh air and healthy food, and some sanitariums (health resorts) treated tuberculosis patients.

Niagara County Sanatorium, 5465 Upper Mountain Road, Lockport, 1936.

1908-1918 197

Sanatorium Facts

- Tuberculosis was also called consumption.
- The Niagara Sanatorium (1918) was the twenty-first county hospital in New York State.
- Inmates from the county jail on Niagara Street, Lockport, were assigned duties at the sanatorium.
- All patients and employees had to live on the grounds. Dormitories and houses were provided and cars were provided to leave the facility. Residency was enforced during epidemics.
- Well into the 1940s, the treatment for tuberculosis included fresh air, special diets, and rest.
- Tuberculosis was also called the "white plague" because it caused patients to appear pale.

Niagara Sanatorium, Guillemont Building, 5465 Upper Mountain Road, Lockport, is now called, Mount View Assisted Living, which opened in 2015.

LOCKPORT

NIAGARA SANATORIUM, NIAGARA COUNTY TUBERCULOSIS HOSPITAL (1918): For all classes of cases. *Capacity:*—130. *Rates:*—Niagara County patients pay according to their ability up to $15 per week; those unable to pay receive free treatment. Patients from other counties pay $15 per week. *Superintendent:*—Dr. W. E. Deuel. *Application* should be made to the superintendent.

Excerpt taken from *A Directory of Sanatoria, Hospitals and Day Camps for the Treatment of Tuberculosis in the United States* (1919).

Shaw Building (children's ward) at the Niagara Sanatorium, 5465 Upper Mountain Road, Lockport.

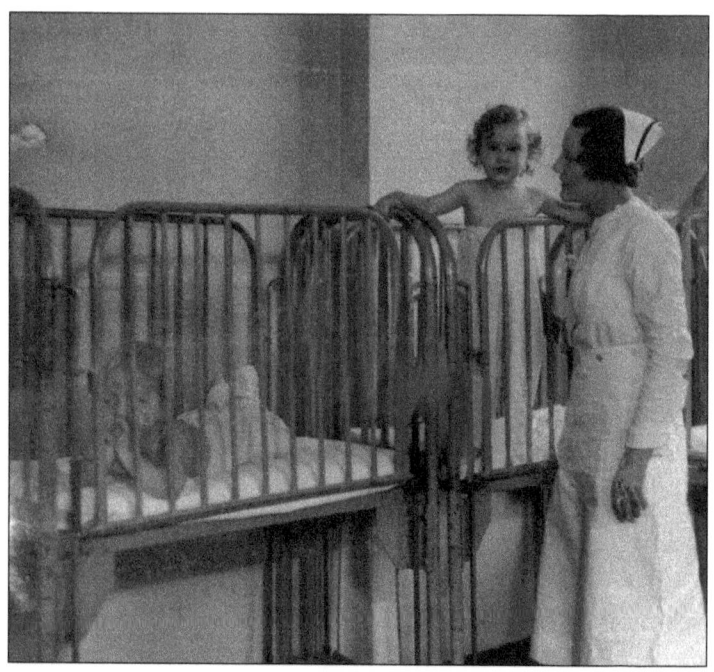
Nurse with children. Shaw Building, 1940s.

Children received healthy meals as part of their treatment for tuberculosis.

Student nurses, Niagara Sanatorium.

Mount View Campus, which is currently for sale.

were located on the east side of Mt. View Hospital. grounds. The facilities provided programs for children from "unstable home situations" according to the *Niagara Falls Gazette*. The homes are now private residences.

The Infirmary Shaw Building was closed in April 1974. Operations at the County Infirmary on Davison Road, now closed, merged with Mount View. By 1978 the 172-bed, long-term care home was established and the name Mount View Health Facility was adopted. Mount View Health Facility, a nursing home, closed in 2007.

The Mount View Campus continues to evolve. In 2015, the Guillemont Building was fully renovated and is now Mount View Assisted Living which is privately owned and operated.

What's there now?

The campus remains occupied with Niagara County offices located in the Shaw Building, including the Niagara County Departments of Health, Mental Health, and Adult Mental Health Clinic Services.

The Two-Day Hospital
The Byron V. Covert
Quarantine Hospital
1918

In 1918 public officials in Lockport were dealing with the local impact of the world-wide influenza epidemic. City businessman Byron V. Covert of the Covert Gear Company, responding to a request from the Board of Health for a quarantine hospital, pledged to build a quarantine annex next to City Hospital in two days. Construction began on a Saturday, and the annex was occupied by patients early the following week. The 24 x 60 foot structure was completed with city sewers, hot water and heating, hardwood floors, and interior wall board supplied by Lockport Upson Board Company.

This amazing two-day addition is not mentioned in any historical publications about the hospital. A newspaper account about the annex noted that "Nothing more to the credit of a citizen of Lockport has occurred here in a long time than this act of mercy for staying the advance of the influenza plague in the city."[13]

City Hospital, main building, Lockport, 1908. The quarantine annex was attached to this building. *Painting by Kathleen S. Giles.*

There was an earlier pest house on the site of the present City Hospital, but it was not suitable for use. Several further additions were made to the hospital and a modern building eventually replaced the City Hospital. It was renamed the Lockport Memorial Hospital.

> **Quarantine Hospital**
> A hospital, also called pest house, where sick people are isolated. Quarantine is a voluntary or compulsory isolation, typically to contain the spread of disease during an epidemic. Such hospitals were used during disease outbreaks to house those afflicted with communicable diseases such as cholera, smallpox, tuberculosis, and influenza.

The Lockport Leader
Published Monthly by the Lockport Board of Commerce

VOLUME 3 — LOCKPORT, N. Y., OCTOBER, 1918 — NUMBER 7

QUARANTINE HOSPITAL. — An annex to the City Hospital to be used as a quarantine hospital during epidemics received more requests in the Program of Work Referendum than any other topic not listed.

The Directors of the Board of Commerce have offered to the Board of Health their co-operation in such ways as may be suggested to them in bringing about the establishment of a permanent quarantine hospital for the city.

Every citizen is certainly grateful to B. V. Covert for providing in two days time, quarantine hospital to care for the influenza patients.

Article taken from the *Lockport Leader*, October 1918.[14]

City Hospital, Lockport, Niagara County, 1908.

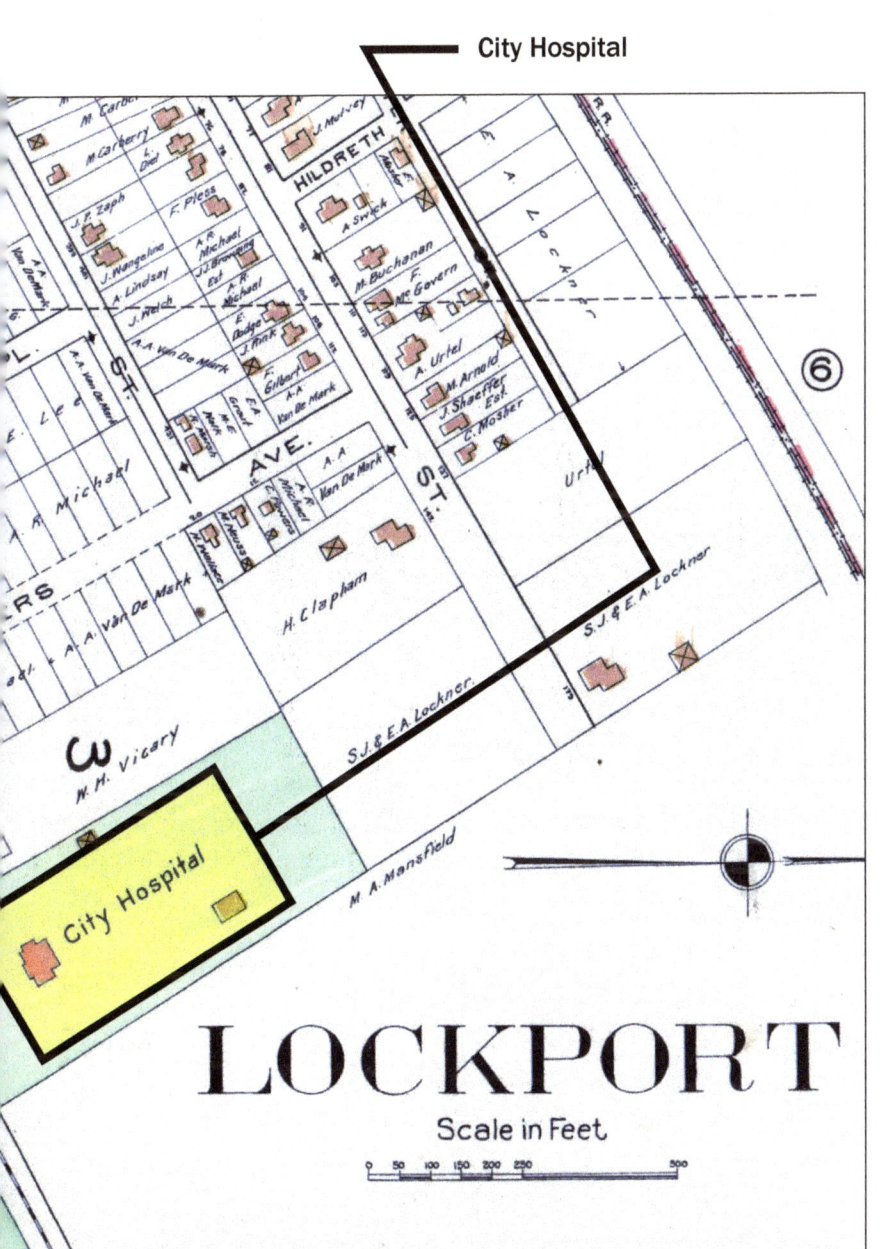

Byron V. Covert was an active Lockport businessman. He started with a bicycle shop at 56 Market Street. On Grand Street, he began to manufacture automobile parts and transmissions. Moving to Richmond Avenue, he produced several models of a car named The Covert. The Historical Society in Wilson, New York, has a Covert in its collection.

The Covert can be viewed at the Historical Society in Wilson, New York.

In *The Turning Wheel: The Story of General Motors through Twenty-Five Years, 1908-1933,* Arthur Pound describes the founding of Harrison Radiator Corporation, Lockport, New York (467-468): "The other officers associated with Mr. Harrison in the founding of Harrison Radiator Company were B. V. Covert, Vice President and Treasurer. Mr. Covert deserves particular notice. His Covert Gear Company made bicycle gears and Mr. Covert himself experimented in motor-car design."

City Hospital, 1920s.

B.V. COVERT MADE GOOD
HOSPITAL ANNEX READY

When Byron V. Covert, of the Covert Gear Company, announced to the Board of Health that, if there was no fund at its command from which to pay at this time for an emergency annex to the City Hospital to care for the influenza patients, for whom no accomodations could be had in the hospital buildings, he would build the annex and would have it ready to turn over for the use of patients within two days there were some who, while they did not question his desire to do so quick a job, doubted a bit the ability of any man to make good on the promise.

But Mr. Covert not only made good; he did more. The new annex was finished yesterday afternoon at 3 o'clock. It was begun on Saturday morning at 11 o'clock. Within the period named a matched frame building, 24 feet by sixty feet had been built; it had been lines as to walls and ceilings with Upson-board; a hardwood floor had been laid; connections had been made with the city sewer system; connections had been made with the hot water system of the hospital laundry and the building had been piped so that heating of the building was provided for; in short, the annex was ready for occupancy.

Today patients are occupying the beds which were promptly moved in and they are receiving just as excellent care as is being given to those who occupy the adjacent main hospital buildings.

Nothing more to the credit of a citizen of Lockport has occured here in a long time than this act of mercy for staying the advance of the influenza plague in the city.

Niagara County Historical Society files, 1918.[15]

The new City Hospital, Lockport, 1949. Most of the old buildings were demolished and a new hospital built on the grounds.

The Lockport Memorial Hospital complex, 521 East Avenue, Lockport. The Hospital closed in 2023.

CHAPTER 4
1920s-1950

The Charity Club
1920's

In the 1920's a Charity Club was organized in Lockport, New York, at 49 Niagara Street. It was a men's club, owned and operated by Lockport businessman O. K. Sharpe. It is not clear what the purpose of this organization was or if any money was raised for charitable purposes. During this time there were successful Charity Clubs in many US cities, usually started by prominent women for the purposes of raising money for local organizations. Most of the activities in these other clubs were Saturday dances with a set fee to enter and an invitation only admittance to select wealthy and distinguished citizens. The similar name led me to investigate this group.

The Lockport club was easy to research as there was a trail of newspaper articles, however most of the history found concerns legal actions involving the alleged gambling and stud poker games at the facility. All men listed as participating in the gaming were reported as acquitted on all accounts. Whatever its history it did survive from 1922 until 1935 with the building sold to

The Charity Club. This is the location at 49 Niagara Street. This newer building is now the processing plant for Lake Effect Ice Cream.

James J. Lynch in 1936. The Lockport Charity Club was closely scrutinized to see if it remotely qualifies as a charity, and despite the name, there was no evidence that the club had any benevolent tendencies.

Niagara County Health Camp
A "Preventorium"
Lockport, New York
1928–1983

The Niagara County Health Camp was established in 1928 by the Health Association of Niagara County as a preventorium for children exposed to tuberculosis and as a camp for unhealthy children.

In 1930 Niagara County purchased the preventorium for $1 and then sought additional funds from the state to remain open. In a Lockport *Union-Sun and Journal* article on November 25, 1930, camp director Iva B. Pascoe boasted, "The camp had operated 46

Preventorium
An institution or building for patients exposed to tuberculosis who did not yet have an active form of the disease. Popular in the early twentieth century, preventoria were designed to isolate these patients from uninfected individuals as well as patients who showed outward symptoms. Philanthropist Nathan Straus opened the first preventorium on Preventorium Road in Lakewood, New Jersey, in 1909.

Niagara County Health Camp, 6724 East High Street, Lockport.

COUNTY WILL TAKE OVER PREVENTORIUM

On recommendation of the preventorium committee, Matthew J. Kaszyca of Niagara Falls, chairman, the supervisors yesterday voted to purchase the preventorium in East High street from the Niagara County Health association for $1. A mortgage of $2,000 and a note of $1,000 outstanding against the property will be taken over by the county.

Agreement to relinquish the property to the county for such a consideration was reached by the health association at a meeting with the preventorium committee at Niagara Falls on Monday. The health association first wanted $10,000 which the supervisors held to be excessive.

The purchase of the preventorium will be financed through the inclusion of $7,000 in the 1931 budget if the preventorium committee recommendations are carried out. Of this, $3,000 will be used to retire the liens against the property. The remaining $4,000 will be used for operating the preventorium in 1931. Another $4,000 in State aid will be sought.

The preventorium project was started by the health association several years ago and recently the county has been contributing $5,000 a year to assist in its operation.

The report of Iva B. Pascoe, director, received yesterday by the board shows that last summer the health camp operated forty-six days and accommodated sixty-seven children. While in camp the children gained an average of 3.58 pounds in weight.

Lockport *Union-Sun and Journal*
November 25, 1930

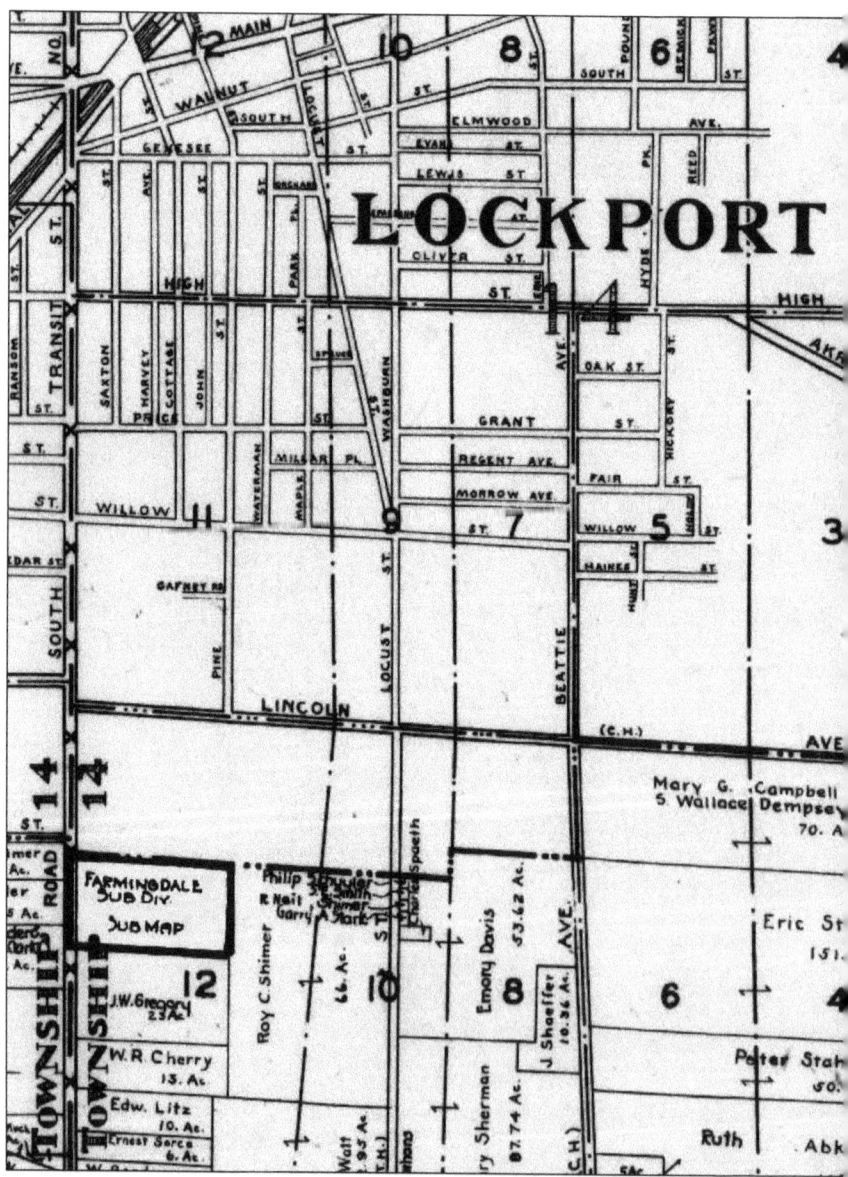

Niagara County Health Camp, 6724 East High Street, Lockport. 1936.

Niagara County Health Camp

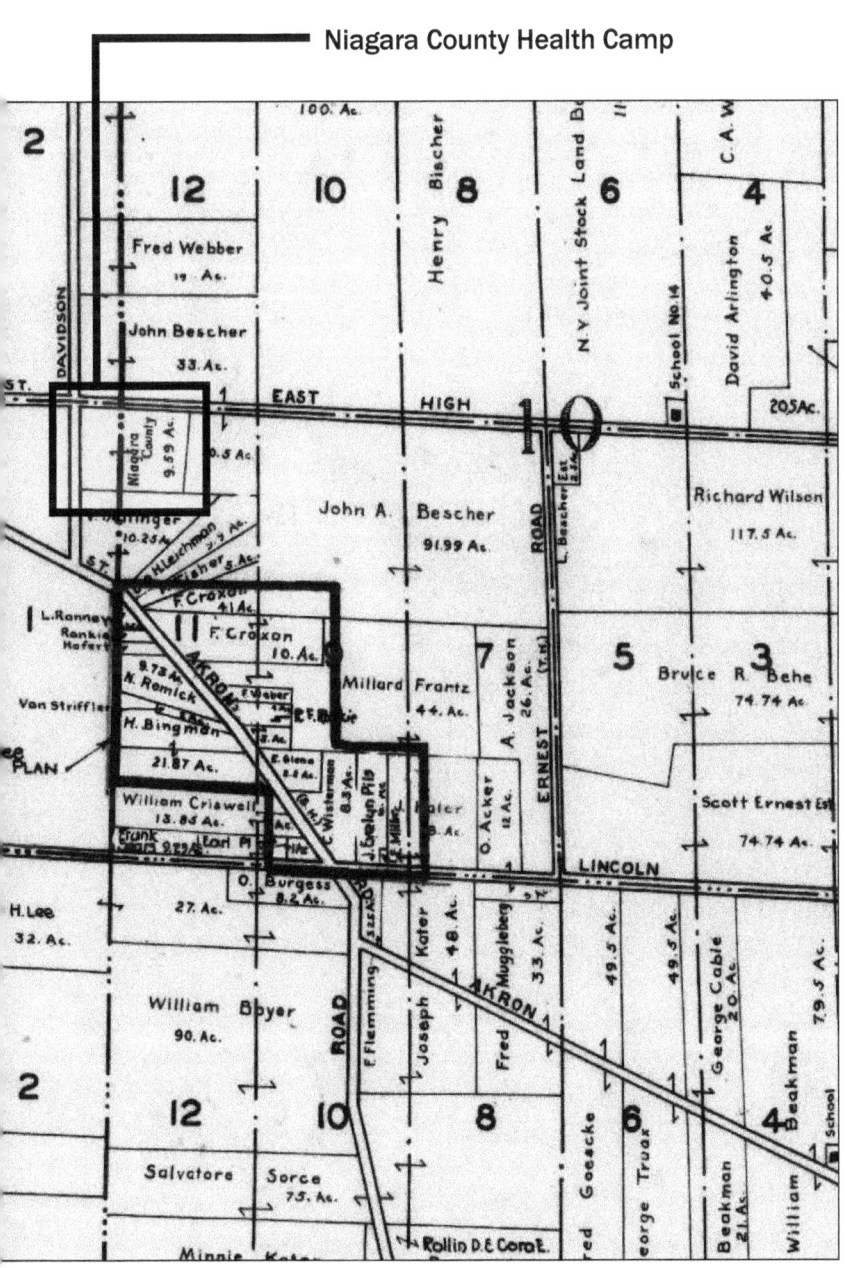

days the previous summer, accommodating 67 children. While in camp the children gained an average of 3.58 pounds in weight."

The camp was built on twenty-five acres of land and had an in-ground swimming pool. There were eleven buildings on the property, eight of which were used to house the children. The camp served thousands of Niagara County children throughout its existence.

In the 1950s Niagara County oversaw operations at what was a summer camp for unhealthy children. Summer camp sessions were conducted with one hundred children participating in each session. Each session included children between the ages of seven and twelve, with forty from Niagara Falls, thirty from North Tonawanda, twenty from Lockport, and ten children from other towns and cities in Niagara County. The children were selected by their school teachers or by county health officials.

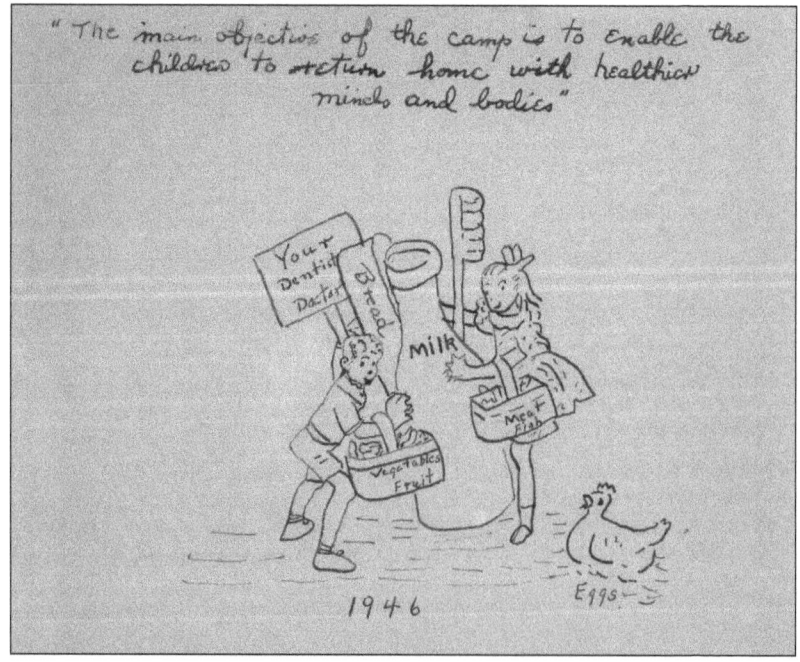

"The main objective of the camp is to enable the children to return home with healthier minds and bodies."

In a September 9, 1982, *Lockport Union-Sun and Journal* article, Niagara County Parks and Recreation Director, Ronald L. Sheisley, reported, "There are four 12-day sessions, each servicing approximately 100 children. The kids are taken on field trips, go horseback riding, go camping, all the things that an underprivileged kid is seldom exposed to. If you could see the faces of these kids, you could see why we are going to fight to keep it open."

> *If you could see the faces of these kids, you could see why we are going to fight to keep it open.*

The Niagara County Health Camp was closed in 1983 due to state code violations. Many of its camp buildings have since been relocated to the county Cooperative Extension and the Newfane Historical Society. Others were dismantled and the wood used to build picnic shelters at Krull Park in Olcott. The caretaker's house was the only building left untouched. In 1986 the property was sold to a developer with the prospect of becoming a housing complex. Today, the former caretaker's brick house is a two-family residence.

Children board camp bus at Niagara Falls City Hall.

The Red House office and caretakers home, 6724 East High Street, Lockport, 1940s.

Campers enjoying fresh air and sunshine.

The "Scrub-a-Dub" washing building.

Niagara County Health Camp.

The County Health Camp on East High Street, ready to be sold in 1983.

The original caretaker's house, 6724 East High Street, Lockport.

St. Mary's Home for Children
A summer home for deaf children
Olcott, New York
1929–1980

A summer home and retreat was purchased in 1929 by the Sisters of St. Joseph of Buffalo, New York. The Sisters also operated St. Mary's School for the Deaf in Buffalo.

St. Mary's on-the-Lake was founded by the Reverend Mother Constantia Driscoll, the Mother General of the order, at the suggestion of convent physician Dr. J. Brady. Brady believed a summer retreat might bolster the health of the children and the teaching nuns against an ongoing tuberculosis epidemic.

"St. Mary's on-the-Lake, at Olcott, on Lake Ontario, is a summer home for deaf children [most of whom were orphans] who do not go to their own homes during the summer," wrote Sister M. Immaculata, SSD, in her memoir *Like a Swarm of Bees*.[1]

Sister Anna Kessen, a children's supervisor at St. Mary's on-the-Lake for ten years, recalls, "I believe the lake house had a thirty-bed capacity. Whenever there were empty spaces during July or August, we would take in children from other regions of the diocese."

St. Mary's Home for Children, 6173 East Lake Road, Olcott. Sold to Le Couteulx St. Mary's Benevolent Society for the Deaf and Dumb on July 19, 1929, and named St. Mary's Home for Children.

Drawing from camp scrapbook.

Only deaf children camped at St. Mary's on-the-Lake in the early years. "They didn't want to mix hearing and deaf children back in those days," said Sister Anna Kessen.

Sister Brigid Mary, a former counselor at St. Joseph's on-the-Lake, recalls, "Many poor and deaf children from New York City were also brought to St. Mary's on-the-Lake. But, mostly, it was the deaf girls who stayed at St. Mary's on-the-Lake."

A camping brochure from the time indicates that deaf girls who had families were also welcome to attend the camp, but for a fee. The rate of $17.50 per week was charged, plus $.40 a week for insurance.

The camp offered swimming, hikes, picnics, crafts, daily calisthenics and television, along with a balanced diet, spiritual development and attention to the children's prayer lives.

"Here many happy hours are passed in relief from the routine of the year's labor, doubly necessary for pupils and teachers in this so strenuous occupation of teaching the deaf to hear and the dumb to speak," said Sister Anna Kessen.[2]

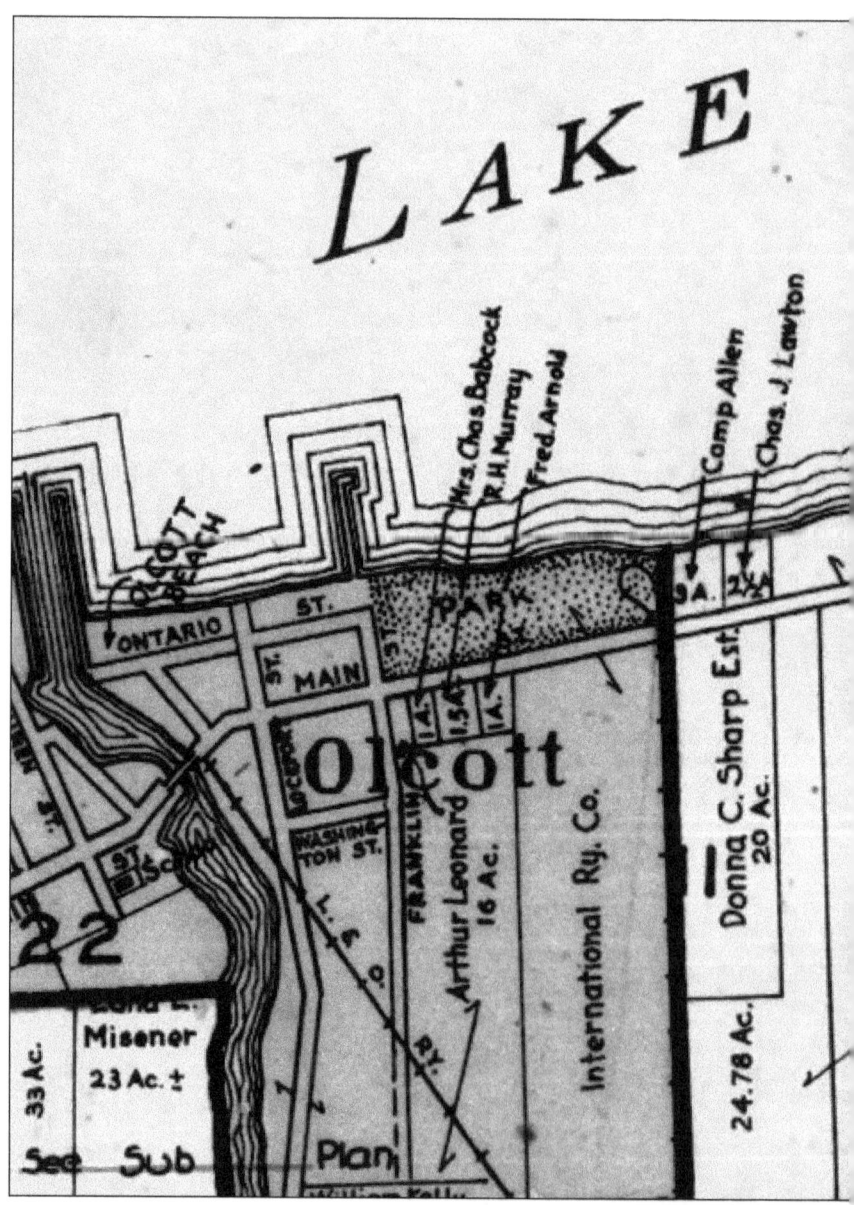

St. Mary's on-the-Lake, summer home for deaf children, Town of Newfane, 1936.

1920s-1950 237

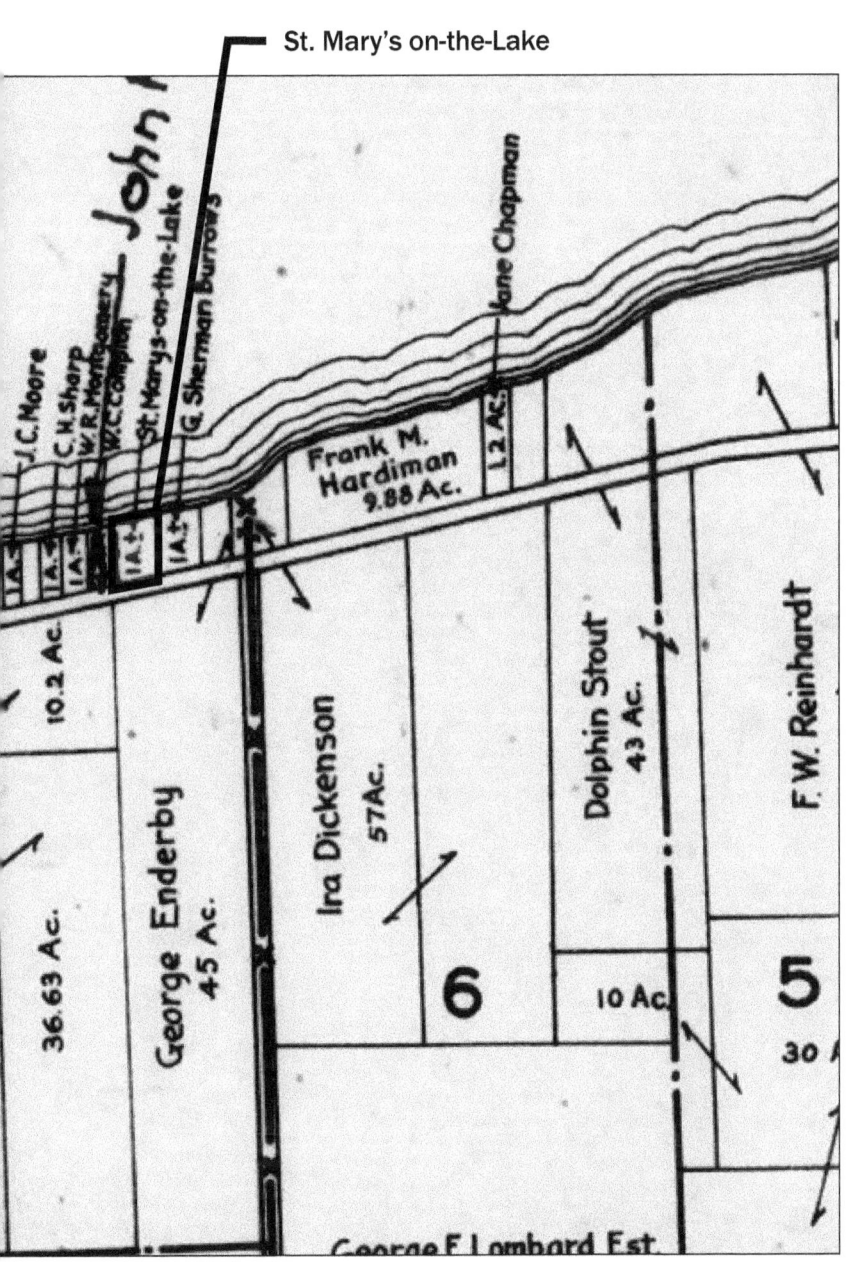

St. Mary's-on-the-Lake House as purchased in 1929.

St. Mary's before the two-story enclosed porches were added as sleeping quarters.

A sewing class for girls.

The bus from Buffalo.

Campers at a picnic.

Swimming in Lake Ontario.

Front view of St. Mary's. Beds can be seen on the fresh air porches.

What's there now?

The home was sold in 1980. Sales records described it as a "home for crippled children." In 1987 the buildings were removed and a private residence built on the property.

The Martha H. Beeman Foundation Child Guidance Clinics Niagara County, New York 1930–1995

The Martha H. Beeman Foundation was created in 1930 in Niagara Falls as a result of a $400,000 bequest by Martha H. Beeman. She desired, "that the money be used in Niagara County for children who were unhappy."

The first office of the clinic was located at 450 Canal Basin, Niagara Falls, in a space provided by the Niagara Falls Hydraulic Power and Manufacturing Company. The Defiance Paper Company of Niagara Falls provided furnishings and Cliff Paper Company provided heat.

Martha Beeman, who did not have children, was married to Marcus H. Beeman, the inventor of Spirella, a substitute for whalebone used in women's garments. Mrs. Beeman was a donor to local charities, especially for the support of needy children. She built a dining room at Wyndham Lawn Orphan Home in Lockport and contributed to the Rotary Club's "Crippled Children Fund."

From 1930 to 1995, the Foundation operated Child Guidance Clinics in Niagara Falls, North Tonawanda, and Lockport. In 1995,

The Beeman Child Guidance Clinic, 650 4th Street, Niagara Falls. This was the first clinic building owned by the Beeman Foundation. The foundation closed the clinic in 1995.

Martha Beeman

> " The money is to be used in Niagara County for children who are unhappy."

Martha Beeman

Niagara Falls Memorial Medical Center took over the child guidance clinic functions.

The Foundation does not operate any programs today—all of its clinics closed in 1995. An April 8, 2011 *Buffalo News* article notes that the Martha H. Beeman Foundation donated all of its money to the United Way of Greater Niagara.

Former Beeman Child Guidance Clinic, 74 Webster Street, North Tonawanda.

What's there now?

Former Beeman Child Guidance Clinic, located at 251 East Avenue, Lockport, is now Lockport Care-Net Pregnancy Center.

St. Francis of Mount Alvernia Orphanage and Care Home
8409 Haight Road, Barker, New York
1931–1979

The Congregation of the Sisters of Saint Felix of Cantalice, or the Felician Sisters of St. Francis, as they were called, focused on the Polish sector of Buffalo, establishing an orphanage there in 1895. The Immaculate Heart of Mary Orphan Home in Cheektowaga was organized for children of immigrant families from Poland who were either disabled or orphaned.

Prompted by demands of the New York State Department of Social Welfare, Mother Angelina, director of the orphan home, began her hunt for a summer camp for the children in the late 1920s.

The Felician Sisters purchased 89.5 acres of farm land from Willis T. Mann for $13,000 in 1931. The land included an orchard with peach and apple trees, a house, a barn, and a park-like area with imported trees from the Holy Land.

A portion of the site was used as a health retreat for nuns who were recuperating from illnesses. In January of 1932, the large, old

Main House, Sisters Convent. Still known locally as the Sisters' House, it is located at 8400 Haight Road, Barker.

Statue of St. Francis on the property.

frame house on the farm was renovated as their convent.

The first camping activities were held in the summer of 1932. The only place to swim was Lake Ontario, two miles away from the camp. "Excitement reigned in the home as the first group of about twenty left for its stay at Mount Alvernia," notes Sister Ellen Marie Kuznicki in her book *Journey in Faith*.

The spiritual development of the campers was overseen by the sisters and the pastor of the local St. Patrick's Parish at the new chapel in Barker. In return, the sisters agreed to conduct religious classes for the Catholic students who attended public schools in Barker.

In the late 1930s friends and supporters of the Sisters organized fund-raising events, lawn fetes, and the Mount Alvernia Club was initiated with weekly card parties held to raise funds for the camp.

In 1945 a day care center was opened for the children of migrant and local mothers doing seasonal work at local canning factories.

The farm was operated with help from the sisters, visiting girls and a few groundskeepers who lived in a small building behind the main house. Johnny Lasak who was called "Johnny Felician Sisters" was the head of the farm crew.

Residents still call it the "Sister's House" and the Sisters were very involved with the local Catholic Church, St. Patrick's, and the Barker community. Peter Devereaux, Somerset Town Historian, remembers their annual lawn fete as a major town event.

From 1932–1953, 1,142 children were treated to a summer camp experience at St. Francis of Mount Alvernia, but the camp became too expensive to run. Because of the lack of access to swimming and other concerns, New York State officials denied the Sisters a license to operate the camp in 1953.

On July 5, 1954, the sisters re-opened the site with a camp modeled on Girl Scout camps in the area, but this time as a camp for girls from the parish schools of Western New York. The new camp operated successfully until the fall of 1976.

One year later, in October of 1977, the convent and surrounding land were sold to the Gordon Bender Bible Institute according to the records at the Town of Somerset Assessor's office. The property across the street was sold in July of 1979 to the Assembly of God church.

Sister Malvina finds time for prayer on the steps of the children's sleeping quarters.

Children playing in the sand.

Sister Gaudentia at Huntington Beach on Lake Ontario.

Johnny Lasak, nicknamed "Johnny Felician Sisters," with children. Dan and Elizabeth Hogan, long-time residents of the Barker area, recalled, "Johnny Felician Sisters was always with the nuns. He rarely left their side. He helped run the farm, chauffeured the nuns and the children around and was their all-around handyman."

Girls watching ducks go into the barns.

What's there now?

The old children's building.

Private home.

St. Mary's School for the Deaf, Vocational Farm School for Boys, Appleton, New York
1933

Appleton Hall was brought to the attention of the Sisters shortly after the purchase of St. Mary's on-the-Lake. The estate, located only four miles down the road from their current retreat house, was comprised of a 117-acre farm, abandoned since 1928, and included two barns, a smokehouse, a log cabin, an old brick mansion, and lake-front property.

"Mother Constantia Driscoll not only promoted the health and well-being of the students and sisters, but she also wanted to provide a source of vocational training for deaf boys from St. Mary's School for the Deaf. To the best of my recollection, when the foreclosed farm property down the road in Appleton was brought to Mother Constantia's attention, she

Mother Constantia Driscoll

St. Joseph's on-the-Lake, 7171 East Lake Road, Appleton.

contemplated whether farming might just be an excellent career training opportunity for the deaf boys" said Sister Cecile Ferland of the Sisters of St. Joseph.

In 1933 St. Mary's Benevolent Society for the Deaf and Dumb purchased Appleton Hall on Lake Ontario, later to be transferred to the Congregation of the Sisters of St. Joseph of Buffalo and renamed St. Joseph's on-the-Lake. Mother Constantia, ever devoted to the children in her care, took a correspondence course in agriculture from Cornell University to learn to properly supervise the farm.

Mr. Sullivan, a local man, and his crew of deaf boys devised an elaborate pumping system to supply water to the main house and the barns. A hidden spring was found on the property that also supplied the house and farm with water and filled a pond now called Spring Lake. In gratitude, a statue was erected to St. Joseph on the bank of Spring Lake that still stands today.

Substantial changes were made to the house to accommodate more beds. A two-story porch was added, giving a brand new look to the former all-brick manor. "The little blue and white chapel

Sister Cecile remembers, "There was a little log cabin at the lake shore that we named Carondelet. We used the cabin as a bathhouse for changing to our bathing suits."

Children swimming with supervision.

Campers swimming in Lake Ontario.

The old barn.

became the warm heart of the house" wrote Sister M. Immaculata in her book *Like a Swarm of Bees*.

In the early years, the deaf boys from St. Mary's School for the Deaf in Buffalo were tutored in farming techniques and working in the orchards by Mr. Rybak, a local gentleman.

> *Mother Constantia, ever devoted to the children in her care, took a correspondence course in agriculture from Cornell University in order to learn to properly supervise the farm.*

The experimental farm was short-lived, as the boys did not adapt well to the hard work of farming. In 1944 a summer home for the deaf boys was established on Java Lake in Wyoming County.

St. Joseph's on-the-Lake became the summer home of the novices and sisters in the late 1930s and was limited to female campers. St. Joseph's on-the-Lake evolved into a summer camp for female students of Buffalo area Catholic schools.

In 1993 St. Joseph's on-the-Lake was sold and the property is now The Winery at Marjim Manor. "The log cabin was sold in the 1960s, cut in two and moved to the south towns to be reconstructed as a hunting cabin" said Margo Sue Bittner, owner of Marjim Manor.

Chapel from the 1950s. This room can still be seen in the main building of Marjim Manor.

What's there now?

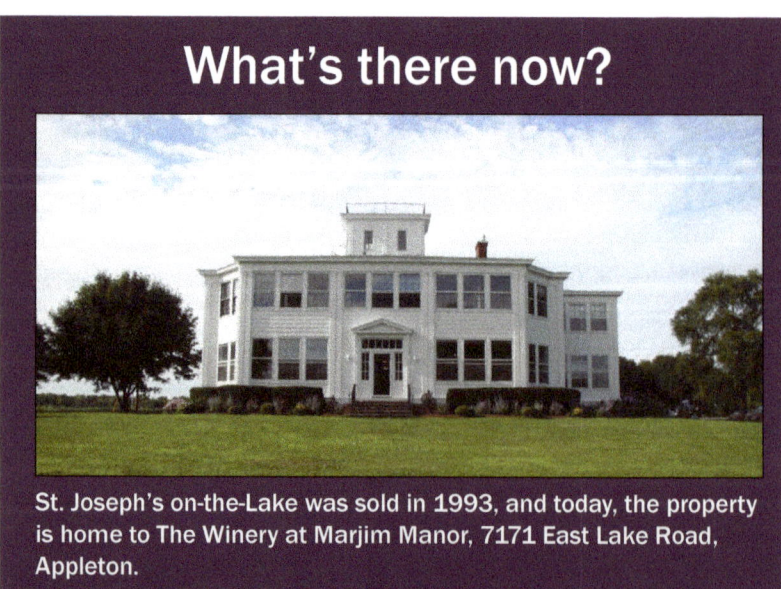

St. Joseph's on-the-Lake was sold in 1993, and today, the property is home to The Winery at Marjim Manor, 7171 East Lake Road, Appleton.

The Boys Home: Barker Residential Boys School 1939

This vocational program started in 1939 when a National Youth Administration (NYA) grand was secured for Barker by Lon MacAdam. NYA was a depression-era federal agency supporting training for young people without a job or in needing of job training. The first residential home was set up at the Sons of Veterans hall on Church Street. Joe Whalen, a famous local artist, was an art teacher and live-in administrator of the training program, which locally was called the "Boys Home." Whalen worked in a continuation of the NYA Program, which phased out in the early 1940's. The new Barker vocational program opened in 1943, with funding from government grants and private pay. A house at 8677 Church Street was secured and became the Barkers Boys Home. Thus began a lengthy and impressive emphasis on vocational training at the Barker Central School District that included mechanics, aviation, and other war-related training for area defense plants. The Barker School District emphasized vocational education for many years until BOCES took over the majority of vocational classes in the 1960's.

Peter Devereaux, Historian, Town of Somerset, Village of Barker at 8677 Church Street, Barker, New York - site of Barker Boys Residence.

> "The job was just not teaching art, it was teaching art in grades, and I want to think third through eighth. And along with that job, I also had a home for boys. Barker had what they called a Center for Boys. It was a reminisce of the NYA. NYA was the National Youth Administration, which was part of the CCC, the WPA, all of that to help kids out and then they send them on to school. These were kids that were having difficulty. I took that over and believe me, I didn't know anything, but they needed someone, and I guess I was the one. I did that job. I lived with the kids, ran the home, and taught the school all day long. I got $2,700 for the year."

Joe Whalen, oral transcript, Lockport NY Public Library, July 23, 2002.

Sunshine League for Retarded Children and Niagara County Chapter of the Association for the Help of Retarded Children
1950–1976

The few public schools that had special classrooms for children with disabilities would only accept children with an IQ of 50 or above. On December 17, 1950, a group of parents of Western New York children at Newark State School organized the Sunshine League for Retarded Children. Their goal was to strengthen support for children with developmental disabilities in institutions, communities, and schools. Working with the Niagara County Chapter of the New York State Association for Retarded Children, Inc. (formed in 1955 and an outgrowth of the Erie-Niagara Association for Retarded Children, Inc.), the Sunshine League addressed the lack of public education for children with developmental disabilities.

Bacon Memorial Presbyterian Church, site of the first school in Niagara County for children with mental retardation who were not qualified for public schools, 166 59th Street, Niagara Falls, 1954.

In 1957 the first Sunshine School held classes in a former Salvation Army building, 67-69 Locust Street, Lockport.

This 1964 poster advertisement was created by the National Association for Retarded Children to increase public awareness of the needs of children with intellectual disabilities.

The second location of the Lockport Sunshine School, 243 Washburn Stroot, Lockport. In September 1974 the school was converted to a workshop for adults with disabilities.

Niagara County Chapter of the Association for the Help of Retarded Children

The first school in Niagara Falls was created in 1954 with eleven pupils in two donated Sunday school rooms at Bacon Memorial Presbyterian Church. In 1956 it served thirty-one individuals, ages five to twenty-four. Several years later the school moved to the 25th Street School, Niagara Falls.

In 1963 the North Tonawanda School was first located at St. Peter's Evangelical and Reformed Church and then moved to the Salvation Army building in the city of Tonawanda.

There was another move to Drake Elementary School in North Tonawanda and then an additional move to the Abiding Savior Lutheran Church, 1534 Ruie Road, North Tonawanda. The final move was to the Ohio Elementary School in North Tonawanda.

The Sunshine League Schools

The Sunshine School in Lockport held its first class in 1957 in the old Salvation Army Citadel Building, 67-69 Locust Street. With the help of local supporters, the Sunshine League for Retarded Children purchased and relocated to a home on 243 Washburn Street in Lockport. The home was transformed into a school house for twenty students, with two classrooms, a recreation room, lavatories, and reception room. Day camps were offered during the summer months, providing students with an opportunity for recreational and physical activities.

In the 1960s the Niagara County Chapter of the Sunshine League merged with the Niagara County Chapter of the Association for the Help of Retarded Children. The Niagara County Chapter of the Association for the Help of Retarded Children

---

By BETH SMITH
Gazette Correspondent

LOCKPORT – The Sunshine Workshop seems to have been appropriately named. Its warmth is not only absorbed by the mentally retarded adults enrolled there, but it emanates from them as well.

The workshop is a satellite work activity center organized under the Niagara County association for Retarded Children. Marilyn Zahler, director of the association, said, "The word children in our title is misleading. We would like to see it changed to citizens, since we actually serve about twice as many adults as children."

The Lockport Workshop organized last September, has five clients from Lockport, Newfane and Olcott, who had previously been at home with no formal program available to them.

Some from this area attend the Niagara Falls center, but it is not possible to enroll them all due to transportation limitations.

Therefore, the Sunshine Workshop opened on Washburn Street in the former Sunshine School for mentally retarded children.

Niagara Falls Gazette, March 6, 1975.

was a member of the New York and national associations.

These early schools for children with disabilities were funded by contributions and organized by volunteers and parents. The schools began in donated spaces, which were quickly outgrown. The schools' programs were closed in 1976 because conditions in New York schools had improved for children with disabilities.

> **IQ**
> Intelligence quotient, or IQ, is a score determined by an individual's performance on a standardized intelligence test compared to the average performance of others of the same age.

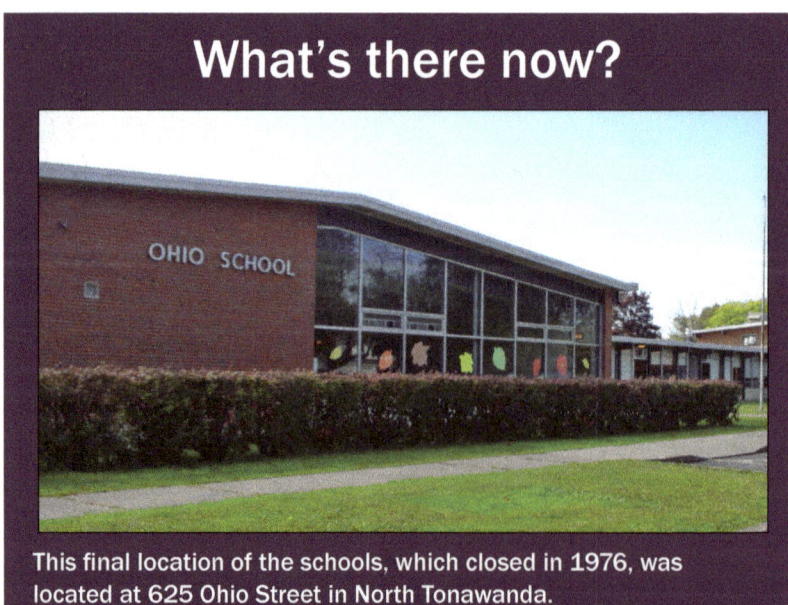

What's there now?

This final location of the schools, which closed in 1976, was located at 625 Ohio Street in North Tonawanda.

CHAPTER 5
Programs Beyond Niagara County

Programs Beyond Niagara County
Large Specialized Institutions

In the 1850s New York State and private groups began to develop programs to provide services to people with specialized needs. Although the poorhouse may have been the first stop for some individuals, many came from their homes directly to institutions. From 1850 onward, poorhouse records reflect the transfer to these facilities.

Better known early institutions are highlighted here, but there were many other options outside of Niagara County after 1850. Because the need was great, there were also a large number of orphan homes.

Large Specialized Institutions Beyond Niagara County

- **NY State School for the Blind**
  Batavia, NY • 1868

- **The LeCouteulx St. Mary's Institution for the Improved Instruction for Deaf Mutes**
  Buffalo, NY • 1857

- **Newark State School (Syracuse Idiot Asylum)**
  Newark, NY • 1854

- **Lime Stone Hill Institutions (Father Baker's Orphanage)**
  Lackawanna, NY • 1851

- **Buffalo Psychiatric Center**
  Buffalo, NY • 1880

Lime Stone Hill Institutions, Father Baker's Orphanage, Lackawanna, 1851.[1]

Lime Stone Hill Institutions

In the mid-1800s in Buffalo, an increasingly large number of children were being orphaned and abandoned. The Diocese of Buffalo, under Bishop Timon, started Limestone Hill Institutions on the outskirts of Buffalo, which included the parish of St. Patrick, an orphanage, and a protectory for young boys. A protectory housed boys considered truant or disobedient, who were then often sent to work on a local farm.

In the greater Buffalo area, only the poorhouse and Limestone Hill Institution would accept African-American children. Because the Institution received no outside help, it was difficult to keep up with the need to expand. The organization was rescued in the 1880s by Father Nelson Baker, who is credited with inventing the concept of direct-mail fund raising, a primary source of funds for the orphanage and school.

Limestone Hill Institutions, now part of Our Lady of Victory Institutions, still provide support to children and their families with a wide range of human service programs.

The New York State School for the Blind, Batavia, 1868.[2]

The New York State School for the Blind

Founded in 1868, the New York State School for the Blind is located in Batavia. As described in a publication of the Charities Laws of the State of New York, 1867, "The primary object of the institution shall be to furnish to the blind children of the state the best known facilities for acquiring a thorough education, and train them in some useful profession or manual art, by means of which they may be enabled to contribute to their own support after leaving the institution." In the early years, the school served blind New York State residents ages five to twenty-one and children of veterans who died or were wounded in the Civil war.

This residential school is now reduced in size, and although still in operation in 2024, many of the needed services are now located in the students' home communities, following the advice of Samuel Gridley Howe, who said at the 1866 laying of the cornerstone for the Batavia school, "I am constantly applied to by teachers to know how to proceed with a blind child; and I always encourage them to keep it at home, and let it go to the common school as long as possible."[3]

New York Asylum for Idiots, Syracuse.

New York Asylum for Idiots

"The New York State Asylum for Idiots admitted its first pupils in 1851. Hervey B. Wilbur, MD, was appointed the first superintendent, and remained in that position until his death in 1883. First located on rented land in Albany, the cornerstone was laid in 1854 for a new building in Syracuse. The first pupils arrived at the asylum in 1855. In 1891 it was officially renamed the Syracuse State Institution for Feeble-Minded Children. After 1900 the name was changed to the Syracuse State School for Mental Defectives and later became just the Syracuse State School. The school also operated a farm and a number of satellite cottages. During the 1970s the Syracuse State School building was torn down and replaced by a residential facility called the Syracuse Developmental Center."[4] In 1998 the last residential building was closed.

Le Couteulx St. Mary's Institution "for the improved instruction for Deaf Mutes," Buffalo, 1857.

Le Couteulx St. Mary's Benevolent Society for the Deaf and Dumb

In September 1853 Bishop Timon incorporated Le Couteulx St. Mary's Benevolent Society for the Deaf and Dumb. A few years later, upon land donated by Mr. Le Couteulx, Bishop Timon moved three existing nearby structures and over time built them up into brick buildings outfitted with dormitories, classrooms, and print shops, thus creating Le Couteulx St. Mary's Institution for the Improved Instruction of the Deaf.

Knowing no sign language, and with just eleven students to start, chaplains recruited missionaries from the Sisters of St. Joseph to come work at the school.

Now called St. Mary's School for the Deaf, the school is still actively educating children with hearing impairments on twenty-three acres at its original location at 2253 Main Street in Buffalo, New York.

Outside Programs 283

Buffalo State Hospital opened in **1880**.

The Buffalo State Asylum for the Insane

The Buffalo State Asylum for the Insane, which opened in 1880, was also known as the State Insane Asylum, the State Lunatic Asylum, Buffalo State Hospital, and Buffalo Psychiatric Center.

The hospital is located at 400 Forest Avenue, in Buffalo. Architects for the hospital modeled it on the "Kirkbride System," developed by Dr. Thomas Kirkbride, an asylum superintendent in the nineteenth century. The hospital utilized "V" shaped patient wards connected to central administration offices. Male and female patients were housed separately, and patients needing less care were located closer to administrative offices. With landscaping by Frederick Law Olmstead, the complex included a large working farm that provided activity for the patients.

The building wards were used until the mid 1970s and the administrative building closed in 1994. The site is now preserved as a historic landmark and the care of patients continues under the direction of the New York State Office of Mental Health, which is housed in newer adjacent buildings.

Notes

Introduction

1. Greg Shaw, *The Welfare Debate*. Santa Barbara, CA: ABC-CLIO, 2007. Describes early care for the poor; a good detailed book of early American charity and its history, 1; 20-35.
2. Patrick Vincent McGreevy, *Stairway to Empire: Lockport, The Erie Canal, and The Shaping of America* Albany, New York: Excelsior Editions, State University of New York Press, 2009. Describes conditions before poorhouses existed, 74; early care, makeshift hospital on the corner of Main and Market Streets in Lockport, NY; Dr. and Mrs. Edna Smith, 82-87.
3. Free Clinic (*Lockport Democrat* advertisement, 1859): "LOCKPORT Dispensary! This institution will be open every Monday, Wednesday and Friday afternoon, from one until three o'clock. At which place the indigent sick can obtain advice, medicines, and treatment, free of cost. Situated in Porter's Block, Main Street, opposite the Big Bridge."

Chapter 1

1. Stephen Katz, *Disciplining Old Age: The Formation of Gerontological Knowledge (Knowledge, Disciplinarity and Beyond)*. Charlottesville, Virginia: University of Virginia Press, 1996. Reviews the history of care for the elderly, including Almshouses and early laws, 50-59.
2. Yates Report, New York's Secretary of State, J.V.N. Yates, was commissioned by the legislature to conduct a survey of public poor relief throughout the state. His report, based mainly upon the replies to questionnaires sent to officials, was first presented to lawmakers in February 1824. The material quoted for this story can be found at http://www.poorhousestory.com/NIAGARA.htm.
3. Memoir of Ruth McGowan Taylor, 1977, Niagara County Historian's records, Lockport, New York.
4. *Suspension Bridge Journal*, Suspension Bridge, New York, July 15, 1882. Newspaper account of the newly built Town Hospital: "The Town Hospital was built on 10 acres of land and had eight rooms, two of which were isolated from the others to serve quarantine purposes."
5. "Frightful Ravages of the Cholera near Niagara Falls," The New York Times, July 26, 1854. "Drs. Hamilton and Hunt repaired to the spot, and found it raging among the Irish laborers, on the Canal and the new grounds at the Suspension Bridge. This afternoon a horrible stench was discovered proceeding from a shanty near a bridge, and it was found to be from the bodies of two men who had died there alone."
6. "The Cholera at the Suspension Bridge is abating today. A number of the shanties erected by the Irish at that place have been burnt down." *The New York Times*, July 25, 1854. Niagara Falls Library, History Center, Niagara Falls, New York.
7. Letter dated December 29, 1980, from I. Richard Reed, Niagara County Historian, to Elton A. Jonas concerning the location of the Pest House Cemetery. Niagara County Historian's Office files, Lockport, New York.
8. A Letter to Mr. Lewis, Niagara County Historian, 1960, from

Mrs. Walter E. Smith of Purdy Road, Lockport, stated the Pest House was located on the south side of Niagara Street Extension where the new jail is located. Niagara County Historian's Office, Poor House files.

9. Niagara County Historian's Office and the Niagara County Historical Society believe the remains were interred at the county-owned cemetery at the Niagara County Infirmary on Davison Road in Lockport, NY. Although Cold Springs and Glenwood cemeteries do not have a record of the burials, and the infirmary cemetery does not have complete records for this period, the papers of Clarence O. Lewis at the Niagara Historical Society, and the Niagara County Historian's Office record that the last burial at the infirmary was in 1960.

10. Niagara Falls Library, History Center, Niagara Falls, New York.

11. Museum of disABILITY History, Buffalo, New York. The names on the board are as follows:

    1865 Charles N. Allen
    1866 Jefferson D.W.
    1867 Frederick
    1868 Wm. S.C.
    1869 Wm. S.C.
    1870 Butler
    1871 Herbert P. Bissell
    1872 Robert Looney Jr.
    1873 Robert Looney Jr.
    1874 Henry L. Smyth
    1878 Charles H. Keep
    1879 Henry L. Smyth
    1880 Frank A. Harrington
    1881 W. Pierrepont White
    1882 James Thomas Low
    1883 Frederick S. Oliver
    1884 William E. Morris
    1885 Carleton W. Pease
    1886 Charles M. Tucker
    1887 Francis Allen

12. Oberlin College records show P. H. Skinner was enrolled in the Preparatory Department at Oberlin College from 1843 to 1846.

13. Dr. Platt H. Skinner's office was at 683 Broadway Ave. in New York City; this is also the address listed for the publisher of both pamphlets. He is listed as a dentist in Trow's Business Directory in New York City, 1854-55.

14. Platt H. Skinner is married to Jerusha M. Hills by Rev. Thomas Gallaudet. *The New York Times*, July 13, 1854.

15. *Before They Could Vote, American Women's Autobiographical*

Writing (1818-1919). Edited by Sidonie Smith and Julia Watson. Madison: University of Wisconsin Press, 2006.
16. In 1858 Dr. Skinner's school was located at 26 Lewiston Avenue, Niagara Falls, New York, above a grocery store. The street name and address have changed, and the former school location is now approximately 1810 Main St.
17. Michael Boston, "Dr. P. H. Skinner: Controversial Educator of the Deaf, Blind, and Mute, and Niagara Falls, New York, Abolitionist," *Afro-Americans in New York Life and History*, 29, no. 2, (2005).

Chapter 2

1. The Home for the Friendless movement was started by the American Female Guardian Society, 24 Beekman Street, New York City. Many "Homes for the Friendless" were started across America. The newsletters of the American Female Guardian Society (1850s) have listings of donations, life memberships, and letters from Lockport residents.
2. "History of Lockport, New York (part 3)." From *Landmarks of Niagara County*, 1987 (see bibliography).
3. Charity Organization Societies were formed in many cities from the 1880s into the 1920s. Many progressed and became service organizations or were folded into early versions of the Community chest and United Way. Charity Organization Societies were "scientific" efforts to eliminate poverty and enhance family life. An early clearinghouse for care in communities, the organization's primary goal was coordinating charity in an assigned region.
4. The King's Daughter is a women's charity group started in New York City, 1886 – Now headquartered in Chautauqua, New York.
5. Charities in Buffalo scrapbook, Buffalo Public Library, Grosevenor Reference Room, Buffalo, New York.
6. City Directories, Buffalo Public Library, Grosvenor Reference Room, Buffalo, New York.
7. *Ibid.*

8. *Ibid.*
9. *Ibid.*
10. From "Our History," Family and Children's Service of Niagara, Inc., at www.niagarafamily.org/history.
11. Niagara Falls Library, History Center, Niagara Falls, NY.

Chapter 3
1. Sisters of St. Francis scrapbook, copy on CD at Museum of disABILITY History, Buffalo, New York.
2. State of New York, State Commission in Lunacy, Annual Report, 10/1/1909 – 9/30/1910.
3. Report of the Buffalo State Hospital to the State Commission in Lunacy for the year ending in September 30, 1909.
4. Tom Kerr, www.fishinghistory.com Fishing Equipment Expert.
5. Tonawanda Evening News, North Tonawanda, Friday April, 8, 1910.
6. *Ibid.*
7. Report of the Buffalo State Hospital to the State Commission in Lunacy for the year ending in September 30, 1909.
8. Forty-First Annual Report of the Buffalo State Hospital to the State Commission in Lunacy for the year ending September 30, 1911.
9. Public Papers of Charles E. Hughes, Governor 1910.
10. Forty-Second Annual Report of the Buffalo State Hospital to the State Hospital Commission for the year ending September 30, 1912.
11. The Buffalo State Hospital Farm Colony had many names here are a number from newspapers and State documents.
    A. Wilson Farm Colony
    B. The Colony at Wilson
    C. The Wilson Farm and Cottage
    D. The Lakeside Colony
    E. The Buffalo State Hospital Annex, Wilson, NY
    F. The Cottage at Wilson

G. The Cottage For Patients
H. The Summer Cottage
I. The Lakeside Convalescent Home
12. Richardson Olmstead Complex Cultural Landscape Report – CHAPTER III: BUFFALO ASYLUM OLMSTEAD VAUX LANDSCAPE HISTORY & EVOLUTION: Heritage Landscapes, October 2008, Wilson Farm Colony, Buffalo State Hospital.
13. "B.V. Covert Made Good Hospital Annex Ready," 1918, Lockport, New York. Niagara County History Museum, Lockport, New York, B.V. Covert file.
14. "Quarantine Hospital," *The Lockport Leader*, October 1918. Niagara County History Museum, Lockport, New York, B.V. Covert file.
15. "B.V. Covert Made Good Hospital Annex Ready," 1918, Lockport, New York. Niagara County History Museum, Lockport, New York, B.V. Covert file.

Chapter 4

1. Sister M. Immaculata, SSD, *Like a Swarm of Bees*, pp. 180-181, 1957.
2. Sister M. Immaculata, SSD, quoting Sister Anna Kessen in *The Congregation of St. Joseph of Buffalo* (Buffalo, New York: Holling Press, 1934).

Chapter 5

1. Father Baker's Orphanage (now Baker Victory Services). Photos from Buffalo Orphanage Studies at http://pub4.bravenet.com/photocenter/album.php?usernum=295528492#bn-photocenter-1-1-295528492/56906/1/. Information about Limestone Hill Institutions is located at the Museum of disABILITY History, Buffalo, New York.

2. Historical information about the New York State School for the Blind can be found at http://www.p12.nysed.gov/specialed/nyssb/history, http://nfb.org/Images/nfb/Publications/fr/fr14/fr04se25.htm, and at the Museum of disABILITY History, Buffalo, New York.
3. From an address delivered September 6, 1866, Museum of disABILITY History files.
4. Historical information about the New York State Asylum for Idiots is found in numerous sources, including an early historical account, *The Gazetteer of New York State, 1859*, by J. H. French. Also, documents of the Assembly of the State of New York, Volume 6. New York, New York: New York State Legislature Assembly, 1888, at http:/books.google.com/books.

292 Acknowledgements

Acknowledgements

We are indebted to many who contributed their expertise and knowledge as we researched early helping programs in Niagara County. Over the course of our research, we benefited from numerous resources provided by local historical societies, historians, and libraries. We are grateful for the use of personal artifacts, photographs, and personal biographies and reminiscences shared with us.

The Museum of disAbility History operated from 1998 until 2022. It was located in Amherst, New York - a suburb of Buffalo New York. Many books, articles and papers used the archive of the museum for reference. The archives for the museum were transferred to the Viscardi Center in Albertson, New York. The Viscardi Center is scheduled to open the new Museum of Disability History in the fall of 2025 and is now in a transitional period organizing the museum and cataloguing the transferred archives. As noted, James M. Boles has some records in his files.

Bill Abel, Lockport, New York
Cinnea Barto, Joseph Barto, Oakwood Cemetery Association, Niagara Falls, New York
Beeman Foundation, Niagara Falls, New York
Mary Bohmhauer, Buffalo, New York
Michael Boston, PhD, Brockport State College, Brockport, New York
Amy Bryan, Lockport, New York
Earl W. Brydges, Esq., Lewiston, New York
Buffalo and Erie County Historical Research Library, Buffalo, New York
Buffalo and Erie County Historical Society, Buffalo, New York
Chris Carlin, historian, Niagara County Sheriff's Office, Lockport, New York
Dr. Albert Cavallari, Lockport, New York
Maureen Fennie Collura, Niagara Falls Public Library, Niagara Falls, New York
Judith Dingeldey, historian, Newfane, New York
Melissa Dunlap, director, Niagara County Historical Society, Lockport, New York
Reid Dunlavey, Museum of disABILITY History, Buffalo, New York
Eckerson, Nancy, Akron Town Historian, Akron, New York.
Catherine L. Emerson, Craig E. Bacon, Ronald F. Cary, Niagara County Historian's Office, Lockport, New York
Douglas V. Farley, History Center, Niagara County Historical Society, Inc., Lockport, New York
Brooke Genter, historian, Cambria, New York
Tom Glair, Batavia, New York
Michelle Green, People Inc.
Pam Groff and Frank Gallagher, Wilson Historical Society
Ken Grossi, Oberlin College, Oberlin, Ohio
Larry Hasley, historian, Town of Lockport, New York
Pam Hauth, executive director, Lewiston Historical Association,

Lewiston, New York
Ulf Hedberg, Gallaudet University, Washington, D.C.
Charles Horton, Wilson NY Historian (Ret.)
Wayne F. Jagow, Niagara County Clerk, Lockport, New York
Tom Kelleher, Old Sturbridge Village Research Library, Sturbridge, Massachusetts
Ann Marie Linnabery, Niagara County Historical Society, Lockport, New York
Parke Morrow, Jr. and Jeffrey Scott Morrow, The Book Corner, Niagara Falls, New York
New Jersey School for the Deaf, Trenton, New Jersey
New York State Library, Albany, New York
Niagara County Genealogical Society, Lockport, New York
Niagara County Historical Society, Lockport, New York
Niagara Falls Library, Local History Department, Niagara Falls, New York
Gary Nigh, Trenton Historical Society, Trenton, New Jersey
Brian Pietrus, intern, Buffalo State College, Buffalo, New York
Becky Pitter, Odd Fellows, Lockport, New York
Doug Platt, Museum of disABILITY History, Buffalo, New York
Publications team: Nancy Palumbo, Tess Fraser, Rachel Bridges, Sallie Randolph, Donna Budniewski, Stephanie Kryst
Jeannette Robichaund, Old Sturbridge Village Research Library, Sturbridge, Massachusetts
Melissa Royer, People Inc.
Mr. & Mrs. Tordoff, Wilson, New York
Lorraine Wayner, historian, Town of Somerset, New York
Robert S. Wills, Lockport, New York

Bibliography

Black Education in New York State, From Colonial to Modern Times. Syracuse, New York: Syracuse University Press, 1979.

Boles, James M., and Michael Boston. *Dr. Skinner's Remarkable School for "Colored Deaf, Dumb, and Blind Children.* Buffalo, New York: People Ink Press, 2010.

Boston, Michael. "Dr. P. H. Skinner: Controversial Educator of the Deaf, Blind and Mute, and Niagara Falls, New York, Abolitionist." *Afro-Americans in New York Life and History,* 29 no. 2, 2006.

Brandt, Lillian. "The Charity Organization Society of the City of New York, 1882–1907, History: Account of Present Activities." Twenty-fifth annual report, Sept. 13, 1907.

Charity Organization Review. Vol. 5, January to June 1899. London: Longman's, Green, and Company.

Cole, Donald B. *A Jackson Man, Amos Kendall and the Rise of American Democracy.* Baton Rouge, Louisiana: Louisiana State University Press, 2004.

Daniel, Thomas M. *Captain of Death: The Story of Tuberculosis.* Rochester, New York: University of Rochester Press, 1997.

Dietz, Suzanne Simon. *Lewiston, Images of America.* San Franciso: Arcadia Publishing, 2006.

Felician Sisters of St. Francis. Scrapbook, copy available at Museum of disABILITY History, Buffalo, New York.

"History of Lockport" (part 3). From *Landmarks of Niagara County, New York*. William Pool, editor. Syracuse, New York: D. Mason and Company, 1897.

Katz, Stephen. *Disciplining Old Age: The Formation of Gerontological Knowledge (Knowledge, Disciplinarity and Beyond)*. Charlottesville, Virginia: University of Virginia Press, 1996. Reviews the history of care for the elderly, including almshouses and early laws.

Taylor, Ruth McGowan. Memoir, Niagara County Historian's records, Lockport, New York, 1977.

Immaculata, Sister M., SSD, *Like a Swarm of Bees*. Published by Mt. St. Joseph, Buffalo, New York, 1957.

McGreevy, Patrick Vincent. *Stairway to Empire: Lockport, The Erie Canal, and The Shaping of America*. Albany, New York: Excelsior Editions, State University of New York Press, 2009. Describes conditions before poorhouses existed and early care for the needy.

Shaw, Greg. *The Welfare Debate*. Santa Barbara, CA: ABC-CLIO, 2007. Describes early care for the poor; a good detailed book of early American charity and its history.

Sisters of St. Joseph. Scrapbook, copy available at Museum of disABILITY History, Buffalo, New York.

Definitions

Definitions

Note: For historical accuracy, the exact language of the historical periods discussed in this book has been retained. No offense is intended toward any individual or group.

Almshouse – A synonym for poorhouse; a place operated by the local government or a charity to house needy or dependent persons.

Backward – Retarded in mental development.

Consumption – An old name for tuberculosis (TB) that describes how the illness wastes away or consumes its victims. TB is a potentially fatal contagious disease that is mainly an infection in the lungs. Although TB can be treated, cured, and can be prevented if persons at risk take certain drugs, scientists have never completely wiped it out. Few diseases have caused so much distress or claimed so many lives. In the past, treatment of TB was primarily supportive. Patients were kept in isolation, encouraged to rest, and fed well. (http://medical-dictionary.thefreedictionary.com/Consumption+(disease)

Dead House – A structure used for the temporary storage of a human corpse before burial, usually located within or near a cemetery. These were more common before the mid 1900s in areas with cold winters, because grave excavation during the winter was difficult. (Wikipedia)

Delirium Tremens – A severe form of alcohol withdrawal that involves sudden and severe mental or neurological changes.

Destitute – Without means of subsistence, lacking food, clothing, and shelter; completely impoverished. Very Poor.

Disappointment Room – Families with financial means would construct a special room to hide a disabled child or family member. The room was locked on the outside and could include a center drain for human waste.

Dropsy – An old term for the swelling of soft tissue due to the accumulation of excess water. (http://www.medterms.com/script/main/art.asp?articlekey=13311)

Dullard – A stupid or unimaginative person.

Feeble-minded – Mentally deficient.

Fool – A person lacking in judgment or prudence; a harmlessly deranged person or one lacking in common powers of understanding.

Half Orphan – A person, especially a child, with only one living parent. (allwords.com)

Head Money (Head Tax) – Almshouses were required to document whether a resident had paid this tax upon immigration. This tax was implemented by the Immigration Act of 1882 and required 50 cents to be paid for each immigrant entering into the United States. The money was to be used to pay for immigration services.

Idiot – Usually offensive. A person affected with extreme mental retardation; a foolish or stupid person with an IQ of 0-25.

Imbecile – Usually offensive. A person affected with moderate mental retardation (IQ 26-50).

Indoor Relief – Recipients of Indoor Relief were required to live in an Almshouse.

Infirmary – A place where the infirm or sick are lodged for care and treatment.

Insane – Mentally disordered: exhibiting insanity.
Lying in Women – Pregnant women.
Marasmus – Extreme malnutrition and emaciation (especially in children); can result from inadequate intake of food or from malabsorption or metabolic disorders.
Mentally Defective – Refers to a person whose mental defect renders him/her temporarily or permanently incapable of appraising the nature of his/her own conduct.
Mentally Deficient – Below average level of intellectual functioning, usually defined by a low IQ, combined with limitations in the skills necessary for daily living. Daily living skills include such things as communication, the ability to care for oneself, and the ability to work.
Mongoloid – Term for a mentally retarded person. Once used to denote people with Down's syndrome, it is now considered derogatory.
Moral Imbecile – "Moral imbecility," also referred to as juvenile insanity, moral insanity, physical epilepsy, and moral paranoia, was a broad concept that included everything from minor behavior problems to serious aggressiveness. Persons placed in this category were also called "defective delinquents."
Moron - Usually offensive. A person affected with mild mental retardation; a very stupid person (IQ 51-70).
Outdoor Relief – Assistance, in the form of money, food, clothing or goods, given to alleviate poverty without the requirement that the recipient enter an institution. In contrast, recipients of indoor relief were required to enter a workhouse or poorhouse.
Penury – Extreme poverty or economic hardship.
Pest House – An early, hospital-like place where sick people were quarantined, especially used during a plague, to house those afflicted with communicable diseases such as cholera, smallpox, tuberculosis and influenza; a shelter or hospital for those infected with a pestilential or contagious disease.

Poorhouse – A synonym for almshouse; a place maintained to house needy or dependent persons, operated by the local government or a charity.

Potters Field – Graveyard for the poor buried at public expense.

Preventorium – An institution or building for patients exposed to tuberculosis who did not yet have an active form of the disease. Popular in the early 20th century, preventoria were designed to isolate such patients from uninfected individuals as well as from patients who showed outward symptoms. Philanthropist Nathan Straus opened the first preventorium in 1909 on Preventorium Road in Lakewood, New Jersey.

Quarantine Hospital – A Hospital where sick people are quarantined. Quarantine is voluntary or compulsory isolation to contain the spread of disease. It is especially used during a plague to house those afflicted with communicable diseases such as cholera, small pox, tuberculosis and influenza.

Rheumatism – Also called Rheumatic Disorder, is a non-specific term for medical problems affecting the joints and connective tissue. The term "rheumatism" is still used in colloquial speech and historical contexts, but is rarely used in medical or technical literature. Sources dealing with rheumatism tend to focus on arthritis, however arthritis and rheumatism together cover at least 200 different conditions.

Rebekah Lodge – Organized for women, but now open to men and women, Rebekah Lodge is part of the Odd Fellows Order. Members visited the sick and elderly and offered help with daily chores. They were active in the women's suffrage movement.

Sanatarium, Sanitarium – An older word for health resort. Sanitariums often provided fresh air, mineral waters, baths, and healthy food, but some also treated tuberculosis patients.

Sanatorium, Sanitorium – The ending '-torium' generally meant the facility treated patients for tuberculosis. Early tuberculosis hospitals often used health resort-style treatment methods, like fresh air and healthy food.

Senile Gangrene – a form of tissue death caused by deterioration of the blood supply to the extremities in the elderly. (http://www.answers.com/topic/senile-gangrene)

Simpleton – A person lacking in common sense.

Smallpox – An infectious disease unique to humans meaning spotted or "pimple." Smallpox localizes in small blood vessels of the skin and in the mouth and throat. During the 20th century, it is estimated that smallpox was responsible for 300-500 million deaths. Smallpox is the only human infectious disease to have been eradicated. (http://en.wikipedia.org/wiki/Small_pox)

Softening of the Brain – Cerebral softening; a localized softening of the brain substance, due to hemorrhage or inflammation; an abnormal softening of the tissues of the cerebrum characterized by various degrees of mental impairment. (http://www.thefreedictionary.com/softening+of+the+brain)

Worthy and Unworthy Poor – Individuals were judged to be "worthy poor" if they were victims of circumstance, such as widows, orphans and the disabled. Paupers who were seen as irresponsible, who did not want to work, were considered unworthy.

Sources: Wikipedia, allwords.com, medterms.com, thefreedictionary.com, the Museum of disABILITY History, and often a combination of the above.

Illustration and Photo Credits

Illustration and Photo Credits

Artists and Photographers
James Boles; Michelle Brant; Rachel Bridges; Nancy Eckerson; Kathleen S. Giles; David J. LoTempio; Doug Platt; Melissa Royer.

Chapter 1
5: D. G. Beers and Company, 1875. **6-7:** David H. Burr, Rawdon Clark and Company. **12:** J. Boles, 2011. **14:** R. Bridges, 2010. **18:** Museum of disABILITY History, Buffalo, NY. **20-21:** Century Map Company. **22:** Niagara County Historian's Office, Niagara County poorhouse records. **26; 28:** Harvard University's Social Museum Collection at: http://ocp.hul.harvard.edu/immigration/smc.html. **29:** Niagara Frontier Planning Board. **30-31:** William L. Long and Associates, Architects, Buffalo, NY. **33:** J. Boles, 2010. **36:** Museum of disABILITY History. **38:** Young Henry Wells, photo courtesy of Wells College; older Henry Wells, Wells Fargo archives; R. Bridges, 2010. **42:** Niagara County Genealogical Society, reprinted in 1996. **44-45:** Century Map Company. **46:** M. Royer, 2011; N. Eckerson, 2010. **50:** Southern Memorial Association, Lynchburg, Va. **52-53:** Century Map Company. **54:**

D. LoTempio. **57:** Lockport *Union-Sun and Journal.* **58:** R. Bridges, 2010. **59:** D. LoTempio. **60-61:** Century Map Company. **63:** R. Bridges, 2010. **66:** Museum of disABILITY History. **67:** Photo courtesy of Donald E. Loker, DeVeaux Archivist, History Center, Niagara Falls Library. **68-69:** Map by D. G. Beers and Company. **70:** Niagara Falls History Center; Museum of disABILITY History. **71:** Photo courtesy of Donald E. Loker, DeVeaux Archivist, History Center, Niagara Falls Library; R. Bridges, 2010. **72:** Top and bottom photos from National Register nomination form. **73:** R. Bridges, 2010; Niagara Falls History Center. **74:** Rachel Bridges, 2010. **78:** Gallaudet University. **79:** Museum of disABILITY History. **80-81:** D. G. Beers and Company. **83:** Museum of disABILITY History. **84:** Museum of disABILITY History. **86:** R. Bridges, 2010. **89:** J. Boles, 2015.

Chapter 2

94: M. Brant, 2010. **95:** From scrapbook of Ann Bryan and Dr. Cavallari. **96-97:** D. G. Beers and Company. **98:** R. Bridges, 2010. **99:** Files J. Boles. **100-101:** Century Map Company. **102:** Charities in Buffalo scrapbook, Buffalo Public Library, Grosevenor Reference Room, Buffalo, NY. **103:** R. Bridges, 2011. **106:** J. Boles, 2015. **109:** Century Map Company. **112:** Town of Porter Historian's Office, Porter, NY. **113:** *Niagara County Atlas*, Century Map Company, 1908. City Directories, Buffalo Public Library, Grosevenor Reference Room, Buffalo, NY. **114:** Nancy Eckerson, 2010. **122:** J. Boles. **126-127:** Files J. Boles. **128-129:** Century Map, 1908. **130-131:** Files J. Boles. **134:** J. Boles, 2011. **135:** R. Bridges, 2011. **138:** J. Boles, 2011. **144:** Google Maps. **145:** J. Boles, 2011. **148:** Files J. Boles. **150-151:** Century Map Company. **152-153:** Files J. Boles. **154:** R. Bridges, 2010. **158:** Files J. Boles. **160-161:** Century Map Company. **164:** *Niagara Falls Gazette*, undated photograph, Niagara Falls Public Library, Niagara Falls, NY; R. Bridges, 2010.

Illustration and Photo Credits   309

Chapter 3
170: Photo: R. Bridges, 2011. **171:** Courtesy of Sisters of St. Francis and Lewiston, *Images of America* by Suzanne Simon Dietz, 2006. **172:** R. Bridges, 2011. **176:** Report of the Buffalo State Hospital to the State Commission in Lunacy, September 30, 1909; Photo courtesy of Tom Kerr, fishing equipment expert. **177:** R. Bridges, 2014. **178:** Report of the Buffalo State Hospital to the State Commission in Lunacy, September 30, 1909; R. Bridges, 2014. **179:** R. Bridges, 2014. **180:** Report of the Buffalo State Hospital to the State Commission in Lunacy, September 30, 1909; R. Bridges, 2014. **181:** New Century Atlas of Niagara County. **184:** Museum of disABILITY History. **185:** On file at Niagara County Historian's Office, Lockport, NY. **187:** Photo located at Lockport Public Library, Lockport, NY. **189:** D. Platt. **190:** J. Boles, 2010; Michelle Brant, 2010. **194:** Museum of disABILITY History. **196-197:** Niagara Frontier Planning Board. **198-199:** Museum of disABILITY History. **200:** From scrapbook of the period, Niagara County Historian's office, Lockport. **201:** From scrapbook of the period, Niagara County Historian's Office, Lockport; R. Bridges, 2010. **202:** R. Bridges, 2010. **206:** K. Giles. **208-209:** Century Map Company. **210:** J. Boles, 2010. **211:** Museum of disABILITY History. **212:** Museum of disABILITY History; R. Bridges, 2010.

Chapter 4
218: J. Boles. **222:** Photograph from scrapbook donated to the Museum of disABILITY History by Bill Rutland, Lockport, NY. **224-225:** Niagara Frontier Planning Board. **226:** From scrapbook donated to the Museum of disABILITY History by Bill Rutland, Lockport, NY. **227:** *Niagara Falls Gazette*, photo located at the Niagara Falls Library, History section, Niagara Falls. **228-229:** Photographs from scrapbook donated to the Museum of disABILITY History by Bill Rutland, Lockport. **230:** Niagara County Historian's Office, Lockport; R. Bridges, 2010. **234-235:** From scrapbook donated to the Museum of disABILITY History

by Bill Rutland, Lockport. **236-237:** Niagara Frontier Planning Board. **238-239:** Sisters of St. Joseph scrapbook. A copy of the scrapbook is located at the Museum of disABILITY History. **240:** Sisters of St. Joseph scrapbook; N. Eckerson, 2010. **244:** R. Bridges, 2010; Museum of disABILITY History. **245:** R. Bridges, 2010. **248-251:** Felician Sisters of St. Francis scrapbook, Buffalo. **252:** R. Bridges. **255-259:** Sisters of St. Joseph scrapbook. **260:** Sisters of St. Joseph scrapbook; R. Bridges, 2010. **264:** J. Boles. **268:** Bacon Memorial Presbyterian Church. **269:** R. Bridges, 2010; Museum of disABILITY History. **270:** R. Bridges, 2010. **272:** R. Bridges, 2010.

Chapter 5
279-283: Museum of disABILITY History.

Index

Index

A
Abolitionist 79, 85, 87
Almshouse 17, 22, 51
Almshouse law 17
American Express 35
American Female Guardian Society 93
Appleton Hall 255, 257
Aseltine, Sally (Cecelia) LaPlante 154

B
Baker, Father Nelson 279
Beeman Child Guidance Center 244, 245
Beeman Foundation 243, 245
Beeman, Martha H. 243, 244, 245
Bell, Alexander Graham 88
Bergholz 43, 44
Bergholz Holy Ghost Church 43
Bergholz Holy Ghost Church Cemetery 45
Boston, Michael 87
Buffalo State Asylum for the Insane 283

C

Camann, Velma 43
Charity Organization Society 137, 138, 139, 140, 141
Child Guidance Clinics 243, 244, 245
City Hospital 206, 207, 208, 209, 212
Congregation of the Sisters of Saint Felix of Cantalice 247
Covert, Byron V. 210
Covert, Byron V., Two-Day Hospital 205, 211
Crazy yard 19

D

Dead house 56
Destitute 65
DeVeaux College 65, 68, 71, 73, 74
DeVeaux, Judge Samuel 65, 70
DeVeaux School 67, 71
DeVeaux School for Orphan and Destitute Children 65
DeVeaux Woods 67
DeVeaux Woods State Park 67
Diez, Russell 111
Driscoll, Mother Constantia 255, 257, 259

E

Eagle House Hotel 36, 37

F

Falkner, Dr. Lewis W. 111
Falkner, Dr. William J. 112
Family and Children's Service of Niagara, Inc. 137, 140, 143, 144, 145
Family Welfare Society 140, 143
Felician Sisters of St. Francis 247
Felician Sisters of St. Joseph 257
Fort Niagara Hospital 111, 113
Fugitive Slave Act of 1850 85
Fugitive slaves 85

G

Gallaudet, Reverend Thomas 82
Gallaudet University 79
George Rewey 12, 13
German Heritage Museum 46
Guillemont Building 195
Guillemont, Dr. Frank 195

H

Henry Wells Speech School 36
Hills, Jerusha M. 82
Holy Ghost Lutheran Church 44
Home for the Friendless 22, 93, 94, 96, 97, 99, 100, 101

I

Immaculata, Sister M. 259
Independent Order of Odd Fellows 125
Independent Order of Odd Fellows Home 128
Independent Order of Odd Fellows Home Orphanage 128
Infirmary 186
Intelligence quotient 272
IQ 272

K

Kessen, Sister Anna 233, 235

L

Le Couteulx St. Mary's Benevolent Society for the Deaf and Dumb 234, 282
Le Couteulx St. Mary's Institution for the Improved Instruction
 of the Deaf 282
Lewis, Clarence O. 98
Like a Swarm of Bees 259
Limestone Hill Institutions 279
Lockport Ladies Relief Society 93

M

Marjim Manor 259, 260
Martinsville 41, 46
Merritt, Shubal, Sophia, Lewis W. 32
Merritt-Spencer 33
Merritt, S. S. 32
Military cadet school classes, 1935-1936 171

N

New Directions Youth and Family Services 99
New York State Asylum for Idiots 281
New York State School for the Blind 280
Niagara County Almshouse 17, 18, 20, 24, 25, 27, 52
Niagara County chapter of the
    Association for the Help of Retarded Children 271
Niagara County Chapter of the Association for the
    Help of Retarded Children 270
Niagara County Health Association 193
Niagara County Health Camp 221, 224, 225, 226, 227, 228, 229, 230
Niagara County Industrial Farm 28, 29
Niagara County Infirmary 183, 184, 185, 186, 187, 188, 189, 190
Niagara County Jail 23, 28, 31, 57, 58
Niagara County Sanatorium 17, 23, 29, 193, 194, 196, 199, 201, 202
Niagara Falls 59, 63, 77, 80, 87, 138, 226
Niagara Falls Municipal Hospital 157, 159
Niagara Falls Quarantine Hospital 157, 160, 164
Niagara Industrial Prison Farm 23
Niagara Prison Industrial Farm 28
Niagara Sanatorium 195
Niagara Sanatorium (Mount View Hospital) 27
Niagara Sanitorium 30

O

Oakwood Cemetery 59, 63
Oberlin College 79
Odd Fellows 13, 125, 126, 131
Odd Fellows Home 14, 127, 132, 134
Odd Fellows Orphan Home 130, 131, 133

Index 317

Our Lady of Victory Institutions 279
Outdoor relief 11, 13
Overseer of the poor 11

P

Pest house 19, 25, 49, 51, 52, 54, 55, 58, 59, 60, 61, 62, 63
Pest house cemetery 55
Pest House Medical Museum 50
Poorhouse 17, 18, 19, 22, 27, 29, 41, 46, 55, 98
Poorhouse cemetery 30, 33, 56, 57
Poor master 11
Potter's Field 41, 189
Preventorium 221, 223

Q

Quarantine 49, 51, 59, 159, 206, 207
Quarantine hospital 49, 159, 164, 207
Quarry 141

R

Raymond, Colonel 112

S

Sacarissa Odd Fellows Lodge 13, 14
Sanatarium 195
Sanatorium 195, 198
Sanitarium 195
Sanitorium 195
Schoellkopf Hall 74
School for Colored Deaf, Dumb, and Blind Children 77, 80, 84, 85
Shaw, William 195
Sisters of St. Frances 169, 172
Sisters of St. Joseph of Buffalo 233
Skinner, Dr. Platt H. 77, 78, 79, 83, 84, 85, 87, 88
Spencer, Louie 32
Spencer, Louis 32, 33
State Insane Asylum 283

State Lunatic Asylum 283
Stella Niagara 169, 170, 171, 172
St. Francis of Mount Alvernia 250
St. Francis of Mount Alvernia
 Summer Camp 245, 248
St. Joseph's-on-the-Lake 235, 256, 257, 260
St. Martini Evangelical Lutheran Church 42
St. Martini Lutheran Church 41
St. Mary's Home for Children 234
St. Mary's on-the-Lake 233, 235, 236, 237, 238, 240, 255
St. Mary's School for the Deaf 233, 255, 282
St. Mary's School for the Deaf in Buffalo 259
Stoneyard 141
St. Paul Lutheran Church 41
St. Vincent Orphan Home 154
Sunshine League for Retarded Children 263
Sunshine School 269, 270, 271
Suspension Bridge 77, 79, 80, 82, 87
Switzer Building 186
Syracuse State Institution for Feeble-Minded Children 281
Syracuse State School 281

T

Taylor, Ruth McGowan 28
The Mute and the Blind 82, 85
The Winery at Marjim Manor 259, 260
Timon, Bishop 282
Traveler's Service Society 137
Tuberculosis 22, 49, 51, 59, 193, 195, 198, 199, 200, 207
Tuberculosis hospital 193
Tubman, Harriet 86

U

Underground Railroad 85

V

Villa St. Vincent Orphan Home 147, 148, 149, 150, 152, 153, 154

W

Watson, Julia 82
Wells College for Women 35
Wells-Fargo 35
Wells, Henry 35, 38
Wheatfield 46
Widows House 43, 44
Wilson, Sophia 32
Witwe Haus 43
Witwe House 44
Wood Lawn 125, 126
Wyndham Lawn 100, 103
Wyndham Lawn Home 95, 98, 99
Wyndham Lawn Home for Children 93, 99
Wyndham Lawn Orphan Home 101, 243

Y

Yates Report 25

Titles by Jim Boles

These books can be found at your local bookstore and Amazon.com.

No Harm was Done – Alternative Medicine in Niagara Falls, NY

Stories from the Springs – The Niagara Frontier.
Also available in Ebook form

*No Harm Was Done-Alternative Medicine
in Lockport, New York 1830-1930*
Also in Ebook form

When There Were Poor Houses

*Dr. Skinner's, Niagara Falls, New York School for
"Colored Deaf and Dumb, and Blind Children" 1857*

Cures and Care in Niagara County, New York 1830's-1950's

Ivan the Invacar Series: children's books, disability related.

The Gold Cure Institutes of Niagara Falls, NY

Contributed

On The Edge of Town: Almshouses of Western New York -Publisher

No Offense Intended: A Directory of Historical Disability Terms -Editor

Abandoned Asylums of New England: A Photographic Journey, by John Gray -Publisher

Buffalo State Hospital: A History of the Institution in Light and Shadow, published by the Museum of disABILITY History, Buffalo, New York -Publisher, editor

J.N. Adams Memorial Hospital – Her Inside Voice, by Char Szabo-Perricelli, published by the Museum of disABILITY History, Buffalo, New York -Publisher, editor

Buffalo State Psychiatric Hospital: An Inside Report from the 1950s, by Patricia Kautz, published by the Museum of disABILITY History, Buffalo, New York -Contributor

Path to the Institution: The New York State Asylum for Idiots, by Thomas E. Stearns -Executive Editor

Beautiful Children: The Story of Elm Hill School and Home for Feebleminded Children and Youth, by Diana M. Katovirch -Editor

Of Grave Importance: The Restoration of Institutional Cemeteries by David Mack-Hardiman

www.ingramcontent.com/pod-product-compliance
Lightning Source LLC
Chambersburg PA
CBHW062045290426
44109CB00027B/2738